Studies in
Complexity Theory

Ronald V Book (Editor)
University of California at Santa Barbara

Ker-I Ko
University of Houston

Stephen R Mahaney
AT&T Bell Laboratories

Kenneth McAloon
City University of New York

Studies in Complexity Theory

Pitman, London

John Wiley & Sons, Inc., New York, Toronto

PITMAN PUBLISHING LIMITED
128 Long Acre, London WC2E 9AN

A Longman Group Company

First published 1986

Available in the Western Hemisphere from
John Wiley & Sons, Inc.
605 Third Avenue, New York, NY 10158

British Library Cataloguing in Publication Data

Studies in complexity theory.—(Research notes
  in theoretical computer science, ISSN 0286-7534)
  1. Computational complexity
  I. Book, Ronald V.   II. Ker-I
  III. Mahaney, Stephen R.   IV. McAloon, Kenneth
  V. Series
  519.4   QA297
  ISBN 0-273-08755-X (Pitman)
  ISBN 0-470-20293 9 (Wiley)

Reproduced and printed by photolithography
in Great Britain by Biddles Ltd, Guildford

Foreword

Research in theoretical computer science has experienced tremendous growth both in the depth to which older theories have been pursued and also in the number of new problem areas that have arisen. While theoretical computer science is mathematical in nature, its goals include the development of an understanding of the nature of computation as well as the solution of specific problems that arise in the practice of computing.

The purpose of this series of monographs is to make available to the professional community expositions of topics that play an important role in theoretical computer science or that provide bridges with other aspects of computer science and with aspects of mathematics. The scope of the series may be considered to be that represented by the leading journals in the field. The editors intend that the scope will expand as the field grows and welcome submissions from all of those interested in theoretical computer science.

Ronald V. Book
Main Editor

Contents

Preface

Computational complexity theory has been at the leading edge of research in theoretical computer science for the past twenty years. Since Stephen Cook's discovery of NP-complete problems in 1971 and Richard Karp's application of this notion to combinatorial problems in 1972, there has been a continuing surge of activity in this area. It is quite clear that complexity theory will play an important role in theoretical computer science in the future.

Beyond the design and analysis of algorithms for specific combinatorial problems, the primary goal of researchers in this field is to develop a quantitative theory of complexity. Such a theory must provide general results on different measures of computational difficulty (say, time and space), different models of computation (say, sequential and parallel), and different notions of mode of computation (say, the deterministic, non-deterministic, alternating, and probabilistic modes).

It is clear that the $P =? NP$ problem and the open problems that are related to it are fundamentally important in the development of any such quantitative theory of computational complexity. Furthermore, these problems play an important role in considering applications of complexity theory to other areas of mathematics and computer science.

Three aspects of computational complexity theory are described in this volume. The first paper, by Ker-I Ko, describes how the techniques of discrete complexity theory can be used in the study of numerical computation. Professor Ko shows how concepts developed in the study of the $P =? NP$ and related problems can be used as a basis for developing a complexity theory for numerical computation. The second, by Stephen Mahaney, surveys some recent results in the development of a structure theory for complexity classes. In particular,

Dr. Mahaney examines the possibility of sparse sets being complete sets and considers the consequences for the P =? NP and related problems. The third, by Kenneth McAloon, sketches relationships between problems in logic--more specifically, the study of models of arithmetic--and problems in complexity theory. Professor McAloon describes recent research on initial segments of models of arithmetic and shows how certain "bridging theorems" can be used to relate this work to problems related to the P =? NP problem.

These three papers provide insight into aspects of computational complexity theory. It is expected that they can be read as part of advanced lecture courses and seminars as well as by individual researchers.

These papers are based on talks given by the authors at a conference on computational complexity theory held at the University of California at Santa Barbara in March 1983. The conference was supported by the College of Letters and Science at U.C.S.B. and by the National Science Foundation under Grant MCS82-15544.

The preparation of this volume was supported in part by the National Science Foundation under Grant DCR83-12472.

The Editor gratefully acknowledges the efforts of Ms. Leslie Wilson in preparing the entire manuscript for publication.

KER-I KO
Applying techniques of discrete complexity theory to numerical computation

1. INTRODUCTION

The study of formal computational theories of real analysis can be traced back to Turing's pioneering work [91], in which he gave, based on the Turing machine (TM) model, a simple definition of computable real numbers. More studies on the definition of computable real numbers have been done by [85,64,73, 72]. In the 1950's a formal theory of computational analysis, called recursive analysis, was developed in the setting of recursive function theory. In this theory, a computable real function is defined as a recursive functional operating on the Cauchy sequence representations of real numbers [22,23].[1] Many interesting results about the constructive versions of theorems in classical real analysis have been obtained (see [69,70] for a summary).

While recursive analysis is useful in studying the computability problems in the theory of real analysis, it has not been applied to the study of computational complexity of numerical algorithms. Instead, the floating-point model of real computation is often used in the analysis of numerical algorithms, mainly because it behaves closer to the computation in actual digital computers. However, as it is well known (see, for example, [34]), this simplistic model of real computation does not reflect correctly the structure of real computation,

1

and thus cannot be used as a model for a general, mathematical complexity theory. For example, it is difficult to prove, in this model, negative results about the complexity of a numerical problem. In other words, there is a big gap between the theory of recursive analysis and the theory of numerical analysis.

On the other hand, in the discrete theory of computation, such a gap does not exist because of the successful development of an interesting polynomial complexity theory [13,15,31,27,18]. This polynomial complexity theory, especially the NP theory, not only provides powerful tools for classifying the inherent complexity of natural problems, but also reveals interesting mathematical structures of polynomial computation. In addition, this theory has also been widely applied to many subareas of mathematics and computer science [18]. Thus, it is natural to try to extend the polynomial complexity theory to real computation to complement the theories of recursive analysis and numerical analysis. Indeed, such attempts have been made even before the NP theory exists [56,57].

In this paper, we give an overview of a polynomial complexity theory of numerical computation, which was developed in the past five years. Although the computational model and the general setting in this theory follow those of recursive analysis, we use extensively the concepts and techniques of discrete polynomial complexity theory. The main issues to be discussed include the classification of the complexity of basic numerical operations, the relationship among analytical

2

properties, structural properties and complexity properties of real functions, and the relationship between the structures of continuous and discrete objects.

In Section 2, we discuss how to design a general computational model for numerical problems and how to apply the concepts of discrete complexity theory to this model to define computational complexity of real functions. In Section 3, the computational complexity of numerical operations such as roots, integrals and derivatives is discussed. We apply the concepts of the NP theory to these problems and derive lower bounds for these operations which are otherwise difficult to prove in classical numerical analysis. In Section 4, the structure of real numbers and real functions is examined in the context of discrete complexity theory. It is shown that the Dedekind cut representations of real numbers and sparse sets have similar structural properties. From these structural properties, a partial classification of the complexity of NP left cuts in the low hierarchy in NP is given. In Section 4.3 we discuss the relative complexity of real numbers and compare the structures of recursive real functions with various reducibilities on real numbers. Open questions and future research directions are discussed in the final section.

2. MACHINE MODELS AND COMPLEXITY OF REAL FUNCTIONS

In this section we describe our computational model for numerical problems and give the definition of computational complexity of real functions in this model. Our model is an infinite-precision discrete model. It is different from the

3

infinite-precision continuous model, such as the one used by Borodin and Munro [10] in the analysis of complexity of algebraic computation, in which the cost of an arithmetic operation is only one unit. We accept the limit of discrete processing in actual digital computers and will use bit-operation measure of complexity. Our model is also different from the finite-precision discrete model such as the floating-point model because we require a good algorithm to be able to produce outputs with arbitrarily small, a priori bounds. A numerical algorithm in our model works as follows. It accepts, as the first input, a user-specified output precision and, as the second input, an approximate value to a real-valued problem instance with high precision, and it outputs an approximate value to the real-valued solution with the predefined precision. The complexity of such an algorithm is measured as a function of both the size of the problem instance and the output precision.

2.1 Computational Complexity of Real Numbers

In order to discuss computational complexity of real numbers, it is necessary to consider first the representations of real numbers. The most general representations of real numbers include the Cauchy sequence representation, the Dedekind cut representation and the binary (or, decimal) expansion representation. The three representations thus provide three natural definitions of computable real numbers. Let N be the set of all non-negative integers, Z the set of all integers, Q the set of all rationals and R the set of all reals.

4

<u>Definition 2.1(a)</u>. A real number x is <u>computable</u> if there is
a recursive function $\phi : N \longrightarrow Q$, and a recursive function
$\psi : N \longrightarrow N$, such that for all $m, n \in N$, $|\phi(m) - x| \leq 2^{-n}$
whenever $m \geq \psi(n)$.

<u>Definition 2.1(b)</u>. A real number x is <u>computable</u> if the set
$\{r \in Q : r \leq x\}$ is a recursive set of rationals.

<u>Definition 2.1(c)</u>. A real number x is <u>computable</u> if there
exists a recursive function $\phi : N \longrightarrow N$ such that (i) $\phi(n) \in$
$\{0,1\}$ for all $n \geq 1$ and (ii) $x = \phi(0) + \sum_{n=1}^{\infty} \phi(n) \cdot 2^{-n}$.

Robinson [73] was the first to point out that the above
three definitions are equivalent. On the other hand, Specker
[85], Péter [64] and Mostowski [61] noticed that the subrecursive classes of real numbers defined by the three representations are in general not equivalent, and the Cauchy
sequence representation appears to be the most comprehensive
one. In the following we give more precise definitions of
these subrecursive classes of real numbers and discuss their
relations.

First, we need some notation. Let D be the set of dyadic
rational numbers, i.e., the set of all rational numbers which
have finite binary representations. In other words, D =
$\{m/2^n : m \in Z, n \in N\}$. For each $n \in N$, D_n is the set of
all dyadic rational numbers with $\leq n$ bits in the fraction
parts of their binary representations; i.e., $D_n = \{m/2^n :$
$m \in Z\}$. Dyadic rationals will be represented by finite binary
strings (with a decimal point). Let $S = (+|-) (0|1)^* \cdot (0|1)^*$.

We may define a mapping $\iota : S \longrightarrow D$ by

$$\iota(\pm d_n \cdots d_1 d_0 . e_1 \cdots e_m) = \pm \left(\sum_{i=0}^{n} d_i \cdot 2^i + \sum_{j=1}^{m} e_j \cdot 2^{-j} \right).$$

Note that each dyadic rational d in D has infinitely many string representations, each with a different length. Thus, it appears more convenient to use the string representations of d directly in the following discussion. That is, we will write $s \in S$ to denote both the string s and the dyadic rational number $\iota(s)$. For any string $s \in S$, we write $\ell\text{th}(s)$ to denote the length of s.

The set D of dyadic rationals is a dense subset of R with finite representations. Thus, it can replace the set Q of rationals and be used as a basis of a new notation system. We formulate the following representations of real numbers using this notation system.

(a) <u>Cauchy sequence representation</u>. A function $\phi : N \longrightarrow S$ is said to <u>binary converge</u> to a real number x if for each $n \in N$, $\phi(n) \in D_n$ and $|\phi(n) - x| \leq 2^{-n}$. Then, for each real number x there are infinitely many functions binary converging to x. We let $CS(x)$ be the set of all these functions and, for each set C of real numbers, $CS(C) = \bigcup_{x \in C} CS(x)$.

(a') <u>Set representation of Cauchy sequences</u>. Sometimes it is convenient to have a set representation instead of a sequence or a function representation of a real number. We use the "projection" of the representation (a). For each $\phi \in CS(R)$, we define $L_\phi = \{s \in S : s \leq \phi(n)$, where n is the length of the fraction part of $s\}$. We call L_ϕ a (general) left cut of x if $\phi \in CS(x)$, and write $LC(x)$ to denote the set $\{L_\phi : \phi \in CS(x)\}$ and $LC(C)$ to denote $\{L_\phi : \phi \in CS(C)\}$ for any set C of real numbers.

(b) Standard left cut representation. We define $L_x = \{s \in S : s \leq x\}$. Let $\phi(n)$ be the string of the integral part of x plus the decimal point plus the first n bits of the fraction part of the binary expansion of x. Then $\phi \in CS(x)$ and $L_\phi = L_x$. That is, L_x is a special left cut representation in $LC(x)$. The main difference between the standard left cut L_x and an arbitrary left cut L_ϕ of x is that L_x satisfies a pleasant property that for any string s and t in S if $\imath(s) = \imath(t)$ then $s \in L_x \iff t \in L_x$, but this property does not necessarily hold for arbitrary $L_\phi \in LC(x)$. For example, let $x = 1/3 = +.010101 \ldots$. The function ϕ defined by $\phi(2n) = +.01 \ldots 01$ (n 01's) and $\phi(2n+1) = +.01 \ldots 011$ (n 01's and one 1) is in $CS(x)$ and hence $L_\phi \in LC(x)$. We note that $+.011 = \phi(3) \in L_\phi$ but $+.0110 \notin L_\phi$ because $+.0110 > +.0101 = \phi(4)$.

(c) Binary expansion representation. Define $B_x = \{n : n > 0,$ the nth bit of the fraction part of the binary expansion of x is $1\}$. Then $x = I_x \pm \sum_{n \in B_x} 2^{-n}$, where I_x is the integral part of x.

Now we may define various subrecursive classes of real
numbers based on these representations. For example, $\{x \in R :$
there is a recursive function $\phi \in CS(x)\}$ is exactly the class
of computable real numbers defined by Definition 2.1(a), and is
equal to $\{x \in R : L_x$ is recursive$\}$ and $\{x \in R : B_x$ is
recursive$\}$. However, for primitive recursive real numbers,
these definitions are no longer equivalent. That is, $\{x \in R :$
L_x is primitive recursive$\} = \{x \in R : B_x$ is primitive
recursive$\} \neq \{x \in R :$ there is a primitive recursive $\phi \in CS(x)\}$
[85,39]. In fact, this nonequivalence of the three definitions
is a general phenomenon in other similarly defined complexity
classes of real numbers. For example, $\{x \in R : L_x$ is
polynomial-time computable$\} = \{x \in R : B_x$ is polynomial-time
computable$\} \neq \{x \in R :$ there is a $\phi \in CS(x)$ which is
polynomial-time computable$\}$ where inputs to ϕ and B_x are
written in unary notation [39]. It is generally accepted that,
among the three, the Cauchy sequence representation is the most
general one ([23,61,39]; also see the remark following Definition 2.5, and [94]).

In the following we will define the computational complexity
of real numbers using only the Cauchy sequence representation.
We use the time and space complexity of Turing machines [25,26]
to define the time and space complexity of real numbers.

Definition 2.2 [39]. Let $T : N \to N$ be an integer function.
We say that the time (space) complexity of a real number x is
bounded by T if there is a Turing machine M such that the
function ϕ computed by M (i.e., $\phi(n)$ = the output of M

8

on n) binary converges to x, and M halts on input n in $\leq T(n)$ moves (using $\leq T(n)$ cells, respectively).

Intuitively, a real number x has time complexity bounded by T if there is an effective method of finding a dyadic rational d approximating x to within an error 2^{-n} in $T(n)$ steps, or, equivalently, if there is a function $\phi \in CS(x)$ such that its time complexity is bounded by T (where the inputs to ϕ are written in unary notation).

Now we define some interesting complexity classes of real numbers.

Definition 2.3

P_R = {x ∈ R : the time complexity of x is bounded by a polynomial function}.

$PSPACE_R$ = {x ∈ R : the space complexity of x is bounded by a polynomial function}.

A real number x is said to be <u>polynomial time</u> (space) <u>computable</u> if $x \in P_R$ ($x \in PSPACE_R$, respectively).

The class P_R contains all rational numbers, algebraic numbers (Theorem 3.2) and some well known transcendental numbers such as e and π. P_R is a real closed field [39].

2.2 Computational Complexity of Real Functions

Since real numbers are represented by functions (on integers),
a real function is then a functional. Thus a computable real
function can be defined as a recursive functional which satisfies certain continuity properties. More precisely, a (total)
real function $f : R \to R$ is <u>computable</u> if there is a computable functional Φ such that for any $\phi : N \to Q$ and any
$x \in R$, if $|\phi(n) - x| \le 2^{-n}$ for all n then
$|\Phi(\phi)(n) - f(x)| \le 2^{-n}$ for all n [22,23]. (Partial computable real functions whose domains are not closed intervals will
be discussed in Section 2.3.) However, in order to discuss
computational complexity of real functions, we must specify a
general computational model and define computable real functions
in this model. Here we use the function-oracle Turing machine
(oracle TM) as a model [15]. An oracle TM is an ordinary TM
equipped with an additional query tape and two additional
states: the query state and the answer state. When the
machine enters the query state, the oracle, a function f,
replaces the current string s in the query tape by the string
$f(s)$, and puts the machine in the answer state. The whole
process performed by the oracle only costs one time unit.
Intuitively, an oracle TM M computes a real function f in
the following way:

  (1) The input x, represented by some $\phi \in CS(x)$, is given
       to M as an oracle.

  (2) The output precision 2^{-n} is given to M as an input.

  (3) The computation of M usually takes two steps:

10

(i)   M computes, from output precision 2^{-n}, the required input precision 2^{-m}, and

(ii) M queries oracle to get $\phi(m)$ and computes from $\phi(m)$ an output $d \in D_n$ with $|d - f(x)| \leq 2^{-n}$.

This is more precisely stated in the following definition.

Definition 2.4. A real function $f : R \rightarrow R$ is computable if there is an oracle TM M such that for each $x \in R$ and each $\phi \in CS(x)$, the function ψ computed by M with oracle ϕ (i.e., $\psi(n) = M^{\phi}(n)$) is in $CS(f(x))$.

It is easy to verify that Definition 2.4 is equivalent to Grzegorczyk's original definition [22].

One of the most important properties of a computable real function is that a computable real function must be continuous. Furthermore, the modulus of uniform continuity of a computable real function on a compact domain must be computable. In other words, if a modulus function is defined as follows, then each computable real function f on any closed interval [a,b] has a recursive modulus function m.

Definition 2.5. Let f be a continuous function on [a,b]. A function m : N $\rightarrow$ N is said to be a modulus function of f on [a,b] if

$$(\forall\ n \in N)\ (\forall\ x, y \in [a,b])\ [|x - y| \leq 2^{-m(n)} \Longrightarrow$$

$$|f(x) - f(y)| \leq 2^{-n}\ .$$

11

Remark. We note that in Definition 2.4, the oracle $\phi \in$ CS(x) cannot be replaced by the standard left cut L_x or the binary expansion B_x because that would result in the existence of non-continuous computable real functions. For example, the characteristic function of the set $(-\infty, 1]$ can be computed by the following simple algorithm using L_x as an oracle: for any output precision 2^{-n}, simply query L_x whether 1.0 is in L_x and output 0.0 if the answer from L_x is yes and output 1.0 otherwise. This is one of the main reasons that we only use the Cauchy sequence representations of real numbers in the computation of real functions.

Using the oracle TM model and its natural time and space complexity measures, we are now ready to define the time and space complexity of computable real functions. First we note that for a function f with unbounded domain, its modulus of continuity may depend on the value of the input real number and hence the uniform, worst-case complexity of f is not a realistic measure of the difficulty of the computation of f. To avoid this problem, we will consider only real functions defined on the unit interval [0,1].

Definition 2.6 [44]. A function $f : [0,1] \rightarrow R$ is said to have time (space) complexity bounded by a function T if there is an oracle TM M which computes f such that for all $\phi \in$ CS([0,1]), and for all $n \in N$, $M^{\phi}(n)$ (the operation of M on input n with oracle ϕ) halts in $\leq T(n)$ moves (using $\leq T(n)$ cells, respectively).

The time and space complexities of oracle TM's satisfy
Blum's [7] two axioms for complexity measures as well as
Constable's [14] axiom 3 for type 2 functions. Some interesting
theorems in the general complexity theory, such as the speedup
theorem, the gap theorem and the compression theorem [7,9],
have been shown by Kreitz and Weihrauch [47] to hold for real
functions, too.

Definition 2.7. A function $f : [0,1] \to R$ is polynomial time
(space) computable if its time (space) complexity is bounded by
a polynomial function.

The relation between the modulus of continuity and computability of real functions has an analogy at the polynomial time
level. We say a function m is polynomially bounded if there
is a polynomial function p such that $(\forall n \in N)[m(n) \leq p(n)]$.

Theorem 2.1 [44]

(a) If $f : [0,1] \to R$ is polynomial time computable, then
f has a polynomially bounded modulus function.

(b) If f has a polynomially bounded modulus function then
there is an oracle set E such that f is polynomial time
computable relative to E.

From Theorem 2.1, we use $P_{C[0,1]}$ to denote the class of
polynomial time computable real functions on $[0,1]$. In
recursive analysis, a computable real function may be characterized as the limit of piecewise linear functions which have
rational endpoints and converge recursively [80]. The

counterpart of this characterization for the class $P_{C[0,1]}$ is
as follows.

Theorem 2.2 [44]. A real function f is in $P_{C[0,1]}$ iff
there is a sequence $\{f_n\}$ of piecewise linear functions defined
on $[0,1]$, and a polynomial function p such that

   (1) (simple piecewise linearity)

      ($\forall n \in N$) the break points of f_n are in D_n,
      and $f_n(d) \in D_{p(n)}$ if $d \in D_n$;

   (2) (uniform modulus)

      ($\forall n \in N$) ($\forall d \in D_{p(n)} \cap [0,1)$) $|f_n(d) - f_n(d+2^{-p(n)})| \leq$
      2^{-n};

   (3) (polynomial convergence)

      ($\forall n \in N$) ($\forall x \in [0,1]$) $|f_m(x) - f(x)| \leq 2^{-n}$ if
      $m \geq p(n)$; and

   (4) (uniformly polynomial time computability)

      the function

$$g(n,d) = \begin{cases} f_n(d) & \text{if } d \in D_{p(n)} \\ 0 & \text{otherwise} \end{cases}$$

      is polynomial time computable (with n written in unary
      notation).

14

We may also define, based on the above characterization, a slightly different computational model for real functions which avoids the explicit use of an oracle TM [17]. Define two functions $\phi : D \times N \longrightarrow D$ and $m : D \times N \longrightarrow D$ as an approximation-modulus pair if

$$(\forall n) \ (\exists i) \ (\forall d \in D) \ (\forall k) \ [k \geq i \Longrightarrow m(d,k) \geq n].$$

Then we have the following characterization.

Theorem 2.3 [17]. A real function $f : [0,1] \longrightarrow R$ is comput-able iff there is an approximation-modulus pair (ϕ,m), both computable by ordinary deterministic TM's, such that for all $x \in [0,1]$ and $d \in D$, $|\phi(d,n) - f(x)| \leq 2^{-m(d,n)}$ whenever $|d - x| \leq 2^{-n}$. In this case, we say (ϕ,m) approximates f.

In other words, an approximation-modulus pair (ϕ,m) approximates f if ϕ computes an approximate value to $f(x)$ and m computes the output precision of the value $\phi(d,n)$. The class $P_{C[0,1]}$ has a similar characterization.

Theorem 2.4 [17]. A real function f is in $P_{C[0,1]}$ iff there is an approximation-modulus pair (ϕ,m) approximating f, and a polynomial p, such that both ϕ and m are polynomial time computable (with n written in unary notation) and for all $d \in D \cap [0,1]$ and $n \in N$, $m(d,k) \geq n$ for all $k \geq p(n)$.

15

2.3 A More General Approach

In Section 2.2, we defined computable real functions on the unit interval [0,1] and their computational complexity. However, as the computational complexity is defined with respect to the worst-case measure, a simple function with some jump discontinuous points is excluded from the class of computable real functions. Consider, for example, the function $f_0(x) = 1$ if $x \leq 1/2$, $= 0$ otherwise. Although the function f_0 is not recursive, a straightforward algorithm which queries the oracle whether the input is greater than $1/2$ and outputs 0.0 or 1.0 accordingly makes mistakes only on a small portion of inputs and should be considered as a good approximation algorithm with low (average-case) complexity. From this simple observation, it appears that a more general theory of approximation algorithms for partial non-continuous real functions is necessary.

We begin, as an example, with a simple definition of partial computable real functions [44].

<u>Definition 2.8</u>. A function $f : E \longrightarrow R$, where $E \subseteq R$, is <u>partial</u> <u>recursive</u> if there is an oracle TM M such that for all $x \in E$ and for all $\phi \in CS(x)$, $M^\phi \in CS(f(x))$, and for all $\phi \in CS(R-E)$ and for all $n \in N$, $M^\phi(n)$ diverges.

The domains of partial recursive functions may be characterized as recursively enumerable (r.e.) open sets. (A set $E \subseteq R$ is called <u>r.e.</u> <u>open</u> if there is a recursive function $\psi :$ $N \longrightarrow D$ such that $E = \bigcup_{n=0}^{\infty} (\psi(2n), \psi(2n+1))$. It is called

16

recursively open in [49] and [36]. However, it seems the term "r.e. open" is more appropriate as discussed in [38].)

In the above definition, if we allow, for some $\phi \in CS(R-E)$, $M^{\phi}(n)$ to converge (and hence output "incorrect" information) for finitely many $n \in N$, then we may get a more general class of partial computable real functions [47]. However, we choose to take a more general approach. For any set $E \subseteq [0,1]$, let $m^*(E)$ be the outer measure of E.

Definition 2.9. A function $f : E \rightarrow R$, $E \subseteq [0,1]$, is recursively approximable if there is an oracle TM M such that for all $n \in N$,

$$m^*\{x \in E : (\exists \phi \in CS(x))[M^{\phi}(n) \quad \text{diverges}$$
$$\text{or} \quad |M^{\phi}(n) - f(x)| > 2^{-n}]\}$$
$$+ m^*\{x \in [0,1] - E : (\exists \phi \in CS(x))[M^{\phi}(n) \quad \text{converges}]\}$$
$$\leq 2^{-n}.$$

That is, we allow the machine M to have errors but the size of the errors is controlled by the input n. Domains of recursively approximable functions include r.e. open sets (in $[0,1]$) as well as Šanin's [76] and Kreisel and Lacombe's [46] "recursively measurable" sets. (A set $E \subseteq R$ is recursively measurable if there is a recursive function ψ such that for all $n \in N$,

$$\psi(n) = \langle a_1, b_1, \ldots, a_k, b_k \rangle$$

with each a_i and $b_i \in S$ and

$$m^*(E \triangle \bigcup_{i=1}^{k} (a_i, b_i)) \leq 2^{-n}).$$

Indeed, Šanin's [76] and Kreisel and Lacombe's [46] recursively measurable sets can be characterized as sets whose characteristic functions are recursively approximable [38].

Definition 2.10. A function $f : E \rightarrow R$, $E \subseteq [0,1]$, is polynomial time approximable if f is recursively approximable and the oracle TM M in Definition 2.9 for f operates in polynomial time.

Intuitively we may regard this general approach to the complexity of partial and non-continuous functions as a simple formulation of a probabilistic analysis of the average-case complexity (with respect to the Lebesgue measure) of approximation algorithms for real functions. This can be seen from a similar approach taken in discrete complexity theory. In a probabilistic analysis of combinatorial search algorithms for NP-hard problems, Karp [32] introduced the following framework. First, for each problem Π and each size n, a probability distribution S_n over the problem instances of size n is assumed. An algorithm A is said to solve the problem Π almost everywhere (a.e.) if $\sum_{n=1}^{\infty} \Pr\{A$ outputs an erroneous solution on x when x is drawn from $S_n\} < \infty$, and A runs in time $T(n)$ a.e. if $\sum_{n=1}^{\infty} \Pr\{A(x)$ takes more than $T(n)$

moves when x is drawn from S_n} < ∞. Thus a problem Π is considered as a tractable problem with respect to average-case complexity and the distribution {S_n} if there is an algorithm A which solves Π a.e. in time p(n) a.e. for some polynomial p. This comparison provides a sound justification for our approach. (See also [6].)

On the other hand, Definition 2.10 raises an interesting question involved with the complexity analysis of real functions using distribution-independent probabilistic Turing machines [71,19]. First we note that the class of polynomial time approximable functions is strictly bigger than $P_{C[0,1]}$ because it contains functions with discontinuous points and continuous functions without polynomially bounded modulus functions. Let $PA_{C[0,1]}$ be the class of all continuous, polynomial time approximable functions on [0,1] which have polynomially bounded modulus functions. Then obviously $P_{C[0,1]} \subseteq PA_{C[0,1]}$. Whether or not $P_{C[0,1]} = PA_{C[0,1]}$ is not known and appears to be an interesting question because, from the above discussion, this question asks, intuitively, about the relationship between the worst-case complexity and the average-case probabilistic complexity. In [38] it was proved that

$$P_{C[0,1]} = BPP_{C[0,1]} \implies P_{C[0,1]} = PA_{C[0,1]} \implies P = BPP,$$

where "P =? BPP" is a major open question in the NP theory which asks whether a set recognizable by a polynomial time probabilistic TM with bounded two-sided errors is polynomial time computable [19], and "$P_{C[0,1]}$ =? $BPP_{C[0,1]}$" is the question P =? BPP applied to the computation of real functions. This result reduces the question $P_{C[0,1]}$ =? $PA_{C[0,1]}$ to the questions about the complexity of probabilistic TM's. It is not known whether $P = BPP$ implies $P_{C[0,1]} = BPP_{C[0,1]}$.

We remark that the general relationship between the distribution-independent probabilistic approach (using the probabilistic TM model) and the distribution-dependent average-case approach is an important issue in discrete complexity theory which has not yet been fully explored (cf. [96]). The above result, though somewhat depending upon the continuity property of functions in $PA_{C[0,1]}$, indicates a close connection between the two approaches.

3. COMPLEXITY OF NUMERICAL OPERATIONS

In this section we discuss the complexity of some basic numerical problems such as roots, maximization, differentiation, integration and ordinary differential equations. These problems have been studied extensively in classical numerical analysis. Numerous algorithms have been developed in this field. Our approach here is different from the classical approach in two aspects. First, we develop lower bounds for these problems

which are difficult to obtain in the classical approach.
Second, we regard these problems as higher-level discrete
functionals and apply the concepts and techniques of discrete
complexity theory to the lower-bound problems. In discrete
complexity theory, finding nontrivial lower bounds for combinatorial search problems has been one of the major questions
since the 1960's. Since the current proof techniques are not
able to establish deterministic super-polynomial lower bounds
for many apparently intractable problems, nondeterministic and
probabilistic models, space and circuitry complexity, as well
as average-case complexity have been applied to these problems.
Using the concepts of efficient reducibilities and completeness,
lower bounds have been established for these problems under
certain widely accepted assumptions, such as $P \neq NP$, $P \neq$
PSPACE and $NP \neq co\text{-}NP$. (See [18] for hundreds of such problems.) We adopt these proof techniques in the studies here and
obtain similar weak lower bounds for the above-mentioned
numerical operations. For instance, it is shown that the
question of whether a polynomial time computable real function
must have a polynomial time computable integral function is
equivalent to the discrete open question "$P =? \#P$" [17].
This result explains, on the one hand, why all known numerical
integration algorithms are not efficient and, on the other hand,
why there is no proof known for the intractability of the integration problem. Similar results have been obtained for the
maximization problem (related to the $P =? NP$ problem) and the
solutions to ordinary differential equations (related to the

P =? PSPACE problem). For the differentiation problem and the root problem, provable exponential lower bounds have been obtained.

3.1 The Modulus Argument

We first ask, for each of the above-mentioned numerical problems, whether there is a polynomial time algorithm solving these problems. More precisely, let us call a mapping from real functions to real numbers a numerical functional and a mapping from real functions to real functions a numerical operator. Then we ask, for example, whether the numerical functional INTEG, mapping each function f in C[0,1] to its integral $\int_0^1 f$, is polynomial time computable. To answer such questions, we must give a computational model for numerical functionals and operators. Here we use multiple-oracle TM's as a model. Consider, for example, the simple algorithm of using the average of $f(k \cdot 2^{-n})$, $1 \le k \le 2^n$, as the approximate value of INTEG(f). First we must specify how the values $f(k \cdot 2^{-n})$ are given to the oracle TM; or, what the representation of f is. Then we must know how the output precision is controlled. For this problem, it is obvious that the output precision depends on the modulus of continuity of f. Thus, we need to use two oracles in the computation of INTEG(f). The first is a modulus oracle $m : N \longrightarrow N$ which is a modulus function of f. The second is an approximation oracle $\phi : D \times N \longrightarrow N$ satisfying the property that $(\forall d \in D) (\forall k) |\phi(d,k) - f(d)| \le 2^{-k}$. Then the above simple algorithm for INTEG may be expressed as follows.

22

Input.   Output precision n.

Oracles   m,φ

Begin

    k := m(n);

    INTEG := 0;

    for j := 0 to 2^k do

    INTEG := INTEG + $\phi(j \cdot 2^{-k}) \cdot 2^{-k}$

End.

In general, we say a numerical functional F with domain C, a subclass of C[0,1], is computable if there is a two-oracle TM M such that for any f ∈ Domain(F), any oracle functions m and φ, and any input n ∈ N,

$$|M^{m,\phi}(n) - F(f)| \leq 2^{-n}$$

provided that (1) m : N → N is a modulus function of f and (2) φ : D × N → D satisfies the property that

$$(\forall\, d \in D)\ (\forall\, k \in N)\ |\phi(d,k) - f(d)| \leq 2^{-k}.$$

A numerical operator OP maps a real function f to a real function g. Instead of outputing an approximation function ψ for g, we treat OP as a mapping from a real function f and a real number x to a real number g(x). Thus we use a three-oracle TM to compute an operator OP. In addition to the modulus oracle m and the approximation oracle φ for f, we

23

also use a Cauchy sequence oracle ψ for x. We say an operator OP with domain C, a subclass of C[0,1], is <u>computable</u>
if there is a three-oracle TM M such that for any f $\in$
Domain(OP), x $\in$ [0,1], any oracle functions m, ϕ, ψ, and
any input n $\in$ N,

$$|M^{m,\phi,\psi}(n) - OP(f)(x)| \leq 2^{-n}$$

provided that the above conditions (1) and (2) hold and (3)
$\psi \in CS(x)$.

   It is not realistic to define the computational complexity of
a functional or an operator to be simply the worst-case complexity of the oracle TM computing it, because the complexity is
very dependent on the modulus function m. For example, the
integration algorithm above runs in polynomial time if the
modulus oracle m is the logarithm function, but it runs in
exponential time if m is the identity function. Thus, when
we consider the class of polynomial time computable functionals
and operators, we only consider those with domains contained in
PM[0,1] = {f $\in$ C[0,1] : f has a polynomially bounded modulus
function}. Furthermore, the complexity of a functional is
defined dependent on the modulus function m. We say a functional F with domain C $\subseteq$ PM[0,1] is <u>polynomial time</u>
<u>computable</u> if there is an oracle TM M computing F, and a
polynomial p, such that for all oracles m and ϕ represent-
ing a function f $\in$ C and for all input n, M runs in time
p(m(n)). Note that there is no fixed polynomial time bound for

24

M, but for any function f with a polynomial modulus m, M runs in polynomial time. The class of polynomial time operators is similarly defined.

The question of whether a numerical functional or a numerical operator is polynomial time computable usually has a negative answer. For example, the functionals $INTEG(f) = \int_0^1 f$ on $PM[0,1]$ and $MAX(f) = \max\{f(x) : x \in [0,1]\}$ on $PM[0,1]$ are exponential time computable but not polynomial time computable [44].

The proof technique of the above negative results is a simple extension of that of Theorem 2.1. Informally, Theorem 2.1 states that if a function f does not have a polynomially bounded modulus function then, for any polynomial function p, the amount of information obtainable in time $p(n)$ about the input x is not sufficient to determine an approximate value of the output $f(x)$ to within an error 2^{-n}; therefore, f cannot be computed in polynomial time.

This information-oriented argument may be applied to the functional INTEG as follows: For any polynomial p, the information obtainable in time $p(n)$ about a function $f \in PM[0,1]$ is at most $p(n)$ approximate values of $f(x_1)$, $f(x_2)$, $\ldots$, $f(x_{p(n)})$. However, it can easily be seen that for any $f \in PM[0,1]$, there exists a function g in $PM[0,1]$ which has the same polynomial bound as f for its modulus function and the same values as f at $x_1, \ldots, x_{p(n)}$ but

$$\left| \int_0^1 g - \int_0^1 f \right| > 2^{-n}.$$

25

That is, the amount of information obtainable in time $p(n)$ is not sufficient to determine $\int_0^1 f$ within an error 2^{-n}. Therefore, INTEG is not polynomial time computable.

This proof technique has been well known as discussed in Winograd [96]. It can be seen as a simple application of the information-centered theory of Traub, Wasilkowski and Wozniakowski [89]. Miller [57] has formulated a general version of Theorem 2.1 by defining an appropriate "pointwise convergence" topology on PM[0,1], and derived the above negative results as corollaries.

Since most interesting functionals and operators are not polynomial time computable, we ask, in the following sections, the following weaker question: What is the complexity of the outputs of these functionals and operators, if the inputs to them are known to be polynomial time computable?

3.2 Roots

A root of a strictly monotone recursive real function must be recursive [22,42].[2] However, for strictly monotone polynomial time computable functions, the roots may be very hard to compute.

Theorem 3.1 [44]. For any recursive real number $x \in [0,1]$ there is a strictly increasing real function $f \in P_{C[0,1]}$ such that x is the (unique) root of f on $[0,1]$.

Sketch of Proof. The proof technique is a simple "real-valued" version of delayed diagonalization (cf. [51]). If x is a dyadic rational, then the theorem holds (just let $f(y) = y - x$).

26

So, we assume that $x \notin D$. Since x is recursive, we can find, for any $d \in D$, whether $d < x$ or $d > x$ (cf. [72]). We let $f(d) < 0$ or $f(d) > 0$ according to whether $d < x$ or $d > x$, respectively. Thus x is the unique root of f on $[0,1]$. To assure that $f \in P_{C[0,1]}$, we let $|f(d)| \leq 2^{-T}$ where T is the number of moves required by a TM to distinguish d from x. So f is polynomial time computable by the following algorithm:

> For any input $k \in N$, first try to distinguish d from x in k moves. If it succeeds then output 2^{-T} (or, -2^{-T}); otherwise output 0.

Despite the result of Theorem 3.1, many root-finding algorithms exist. The next theorem gives a sufficient condition for functions having polynomial time computable roots.

Theorem 3.2 [44]. Let f be a strinctly increasing function in $P_{C[0,1]}$. If f^{-1} has a polynomially bounded modulus function on the range of f, then f^{-1} on the range of f is polynomial time computable.

A corollary of Theorem 3.2 is that if f is analytic on $[0,1]$ and $f \in P_{C[0,1]}$ then all the roots of f are in P_R. This implies that P_R forms a real closed field.

One of the most interesting questions in recursive analysis is the constructive proofs of the fundamental theorem of algebra. It is known that under an appropriate topology, the mapping from the (complex-valued) coefficients of a polynomial

to its (complex-valued) roots is a recursive function [87].
Moreover, a constructive proof of the fundamental theorem of
algebra given by Rosenbloom [75] shows that this mapping is
exponential time computable. Based on some fast root-finding
algorithms which use algebraic techniques (e.g., [29,95,65]),
we conjecture that this mapping is actually a polynomial time
computable function [44].

3.3 Maximum Values

The functional MAX, defined by $MAX(f) = \max\{f(x) : x \in [0,1]\}$,
is computable on $C[0,1]$. Therefore, the maximum value of a
recursive function in $C[0,1]$ is recursive. On the other hand,
Specker [86] showed the existence of a recursive real function
on $[0,1]$ which does not take its maximum at any recursive
real numbers.

For the class of polynomial time computable functions, the
complexity of their maximum values can be characterized using
the concept of nondeterministic computation. Let P (NP) be
the class of sets which are computable in polynomial time by
deterministic (nondeterministic, respectively) TM's. It is
obvious that $P \subseteq NP$. Whether or not $P = NP$ is a major open
question in discrete complexity theory [15,31,18].

Let us define the class NP_R to be the set of all real
numbers x such that there is a set L in $LC(x) \cap NP$.

Theorem 3.3 [36]. A real number x is in NP_R iff there is a
function $f \in P_{C[0,1]}$ such that $x = \max\{f(y) : 0 \leq y \leq 1\}$.

28

Sketch of Proof. We first consider a discrete version of the theorem. Let $\phi : \{0,1\}^* \longrightarrow \{0,1\}^*$ be a polynomial time computable function. Then, what is the complexity of the function $\psi : \{0\}^* \longrightarrow \{0,1\}^*$ defined by $\psi(0^n) = \max\{\phi(s) : \ell th(x) = n\}$? We reduce this problem to the problem of finding the complexity of the set $B = \{(0^n,t) : t \leq_0 \psi(0^n)\}$, where $\leq_0$ is the lexicographic order on $\{0,1\}^*$. We can easily show that B is in NP. Furthermore, let $B \subseteq \{0\}^* \times \{0,1\}^*$ be a set in NP with the following properties:

(i) $(\exists \text{ polynomial } p)\ (\forall n)\ (\forall t)\ [(0^n,t) \in B \Longrightarrow$
      $\ell th(t) \leq p(n)]$,

(ii) $(\forall n)\ (\forall s)\ (\forall t)\ [s \leq_0 t,\ (0^n,t) \in B \Longrightarrow$
      $(0^n,s) \in B]$.

Then we can find a function $\phi : \{0,1\}^* \longrightarrow \{0,1\}^*$, computable in polynomial time, and a polynomial q, such that $(0^n,t) \in B$ iff $t \leq_0 \max\{\phi(s) : \ell th(s) = q(n)\}$. (We may assume that for each $(0^n,t) \in B$, there is a string u such that tu has length $q(n)$ and u is a witness for $t \in B$. Now, it is sufficient to let $\phi(s)$ be defined as follows: if $s = tu$ with u a witness for $t \in B$ then $\phi(s) = t$, else $\phi(s) = 0$.)

We note that sets satisfying properties (i) and (ii) are similar, in structure, to left cuts of real numbers. (Sets satisfying (i) and (ii) are called weakly p-selective sets. These sets will be discussed in Section 4.2.) Therefore, the theorem can be proved in a similar way as the above proof of the discrete version. First it is easy to check that $f \in P_{C[0,1]}$ implies MAX(f) has a left cut in NP. Conversely, for any $x \in [0,1]$ with a left cut B in NP, we construct a function $f \in P_{C[0,1]}$ such that MAX(f) = x. Roughly speaking, we use the binary expansion of each real number y to determine the value f(y). If the binary expansion of y encodes an infinite sequence of strings $s_1, t_1, s_2, t_2, \ldots,$ each t_i a witness for $s_i \in B$, and $\{s_i\}$ binary converges to a real number z then we define f(y) = z. We note that there must be some real number y whose binary expansion satisfies the above condition and f(y) = x because B is a left cut of x. So, if we can make the values of f at other points y, whose binary expansions do not encode such a sequence, to be less than x, then MAX(f) = x. However, to complete the proof, we need to take care of two details of the construction of f. First, our oracle is in the Cauchy sequence form, instead of the binary expansion form. Second, the values of f(y), where the binary expansion of y does not encode a nice sequence, cannot simply be made to be zero because we need to make sure that f has a polynomially bounded modulus function--as opposed to the situation in the proof of the discrete version. □

Thus the maximum values of polynomial time computable functions are characterized as the class NP_R. But what is the exact complexity of real numbers in NP_R? Let P_1 (NP_1) be the class of sets over a single-letter alphabet which are in P (NP, respectively). Then we have P = NP => P_R = NP_R => P_1 = NP_1 [36]. It is known that P_1 = NP_1 iff EXP = NEXP where

EXP (NEXP) is the class of sets computable by deterministic (nondeterministic, respectively) TM's in exponential time [8]. Thus, EXP $\neq$ NEXP $\Rightarrow$ $P_R \neq NP_R$. Whether the converse of each implication holds is not known. We will discuss more of the realtionship between NP_R and other subclasses of NP in Section 4.

Let MAX2 be the operator which maps each function f in $C[0,1]^2$ to the function MAX2(f), defined by MAX2(f)(x) = max$\{f(x,y) : 0 \leq y \leq 1\}$. Then the complexity of MAX2 can also be characterized by the P =? NP question, as follows.

Theorem 3.4 [17]. The following are equivalent.

(a) Let f : $[0,1]^2 \to [0,1]$ be a polynomial time computable function. Then, the function MAX2(f) is polynomial time computable.

(b) P = NP.

Remark. The time complexity of a two-dimensional function can be defined by extending that of a one-dimensional function in a straightforward manner.

The proof of Theorem 3.4 is a continuous version of the proof of the following result on the discrete maximization problem: The statement that for any polynomial time computable function $\phi : \{0,1\}^* \to \{0,1\}^*$, the maximization function $\psi : \{0,1\}^* \to \{0,1\}^*$, defined by $\psi(s) = \max\{\phi(t) : t \leq_0 s\}$, is also polynomial time computable, is equivalent to P = NP.

3.4   Integrals

It is easily seen that the integral $\int_0^1 f$ of a recursive function f on [0,1] is recursive. We use, again, the concept of nondeterministic computation to characterize the complexity of the integrals of functions in $P_{C[0,1]}$. We call a nondeterministic TM M a <u>counting</u> <u>TM</u> if it has an auxiliary output device that prints in binary notation the number of accepting computations induced by the input. Let #P be the class of functions computed by counting TM's of polynomial time complexity. Let $\#P_1$ be the set of functions in #P which takes inputs in unary notation [92,93]. The relationship between #P and other complexity classes is as follows:

$$P \subseteq NP \subseteq P^{\#P} \subseteq PSPACE$$

where $P^{\#P}$ is the class of sets computable in polynomial time by an oracle TM with a function-oracle in #P and PSPACE is the class of sets accepted by deterministic TM's of polynomial space complexity. None of the above inclusions is known to be proper.

We define $\#P_R$ to be the set of all real numbers x such that there is a function ϕ in $CS(x) \cap \#P_1$.

<u>Theorem 3.5</u> [17]. A real number x is in $\#P_R$ iff there is a function $f \in P_{C[0,1]}$ such that $\int_0^1 f(y) \, dy = x$.

The proof of Theorem 3.5 is similar to that of Theorem 3.3 in the sense that the integration problem can be reduced to the

complexity problem of the following discrete operation: For
any set $A \subseteq \{0,1\}*$, let SUM(A) be a function mapping single-
letter strings in $\{0\}*$ to strings in $\{0,1\}*$ defined by
$SUM(A)(0^n) = \sum \{s \in A : \ell th(s) = n\}$ where the sum of two
strings s and t is the binary representation of the sum of
the two integers represented by s and t with leading zeros
ignored.

It can be checked that if $A \in P$ then $SUM(A) \in \#P_1$, and
that for any $\phi \in \#P_1$, there is a set $A \in P$, and a polynomial
p, such that $SUM(A)(p(n)) = \phi(n)$. Now for any $f \in P_{C[0,1]}$,
$\int_0^1 f$ can be approximated to within an error 2^{-n} by

$$\sum_{i=1}^{2^n} f(t_i) \cdot 2^{-n}$$

where $t_i = i \cdot 2^{-n}$ for $i = 1, \ldots, 2^n$. This provides a natural
reduction of the integration problem to the discrete summation
problem, and hence a proof of Theorem 3.5.

The question $P_R =? \#P_R$ can be shown to be equivalent to
the question $P_1 =? \#P_1$ in discrete complexity theory. Therefore, the complexity of the integrals of polynomial time computable functions has an exact classification in the NP theory.
(This is not true for the case of the maximum values of polynomial time computable functions.)

More generally, the complexity of integral functions of
polynomial time computable functions also has an exact
classification.

Theorem 3.6 [17]. The following are equivalent.

(a)   Let $f \in P_{C[0,1]}$. Then the function $g(x) = \int_0^x f(y) \, dy$ is in $P_{C[0,1]}$.

(b) $P = \#P$.

The above result can also be generalized to the Lebesgue integrals of polynomial time approximable functions (as defined in Section 2.3).

Theorem 3.7 [38]

(a)   A real number x is in $\#P_R$ iff there is a polynomial time approximable function f defined on $[0,1]$ such that $\int_0^1 f = x$.

(b)   The integral functions of polynomial time approximable functions with domains equal to $[0,1]$ are polynomial time computable iff $P = \#P$.

3.5 Derivatives

In recursive analysis, the following results about differentiation have been obtained.

(1)   A recursive function is not necessarily differentiable. Indeed, there exists a nowhere differentiable recursive function on $[0,1]$ [22].

(2)   There exists a recursive function f in $C^1[0,1]$ but f' is not recursive on $[0,1]$ [63]. Moreover, there is a recursive function f in $C^1[0,1]$ but $f'(0)$ is not a recursive real number [68].

(3)   If f is recursive and f'' exists and is continuous on $[0,1]$, then f' is recursive on $[0,1]$ [66].

34

The above results have the following polynomial time analog.

Theorem 3.8 [44]. There exists a function $f \in P_{C[0,1]}$ which is nowhere differentiable on $[0,1]$.

Theorem 3.9 [44]. Let $f \in P_{C[0,1]}$. If f' exists and is continuous on $[0,1]$ and has a polynomially bounded modulus function, then f' is polynomial time computable. As a consequence, f' is polynomial time computable if f'' exists and is continuous on $[0,1]$.

Theorem 3.10 [37,41]. There exists a function $f \in P_{C[0,1]}$ such that f' exists and is continuous on $[0,1]$ but $f'(d)$ is not recursive for all $d \in D \cap (0,1)$.

Sketch of Proof. The proof is a modification of Pour-El and Richard's [68] proof of the result (2) above with an implicit use of delayed diagonalization (cf. Theorem 3.1).

First define a polynomial time computable pulse function g which has the support $[-1,1]$ and has the property that $g(-1) = g(1) = 0$, $g'(-1) = g'(1) = 0$, and $g'(0) = 1$. Let $A \subseteq N$ be an r.e. but nonrecursive set. Define

$$h(x) = \sum_{n \in A} 2^{-(2n+t(n))} \cdot g(2^{t(n)} \cdot x),$$

where $t(n)$ is the number of moves required to recognize $n \in A$. It can be checked that h is polynomial time computable, and $h'(0) = \sum_{n \in A} 2^{-2n}$ is not a recursive real number.

Now we define f as a sum of infinitely many functions h_d, $d \in D$, each h_d being polynomial time computable and having a non-recursive derivative $h_d'(d)$. We make the support of each h_d so small that the difference between $f'(d)$ and $h_d'(d)$ is only a sum of finitely many computable real numbers (of the form $h_e'(d)$, $e \neq d$). Thus $f'(d)$ is not recursive for all $d \in D \cap [0,1]$. □

The computational complexity of some other questions about differentiation has been studied in [37]. In particular, Theorem 3.10 has been generalized to the following: There exists a function $f \in P_{C[0,1]}$ which has a polynomially bounded modulus of absolute continuity such that f' exists and is continuous on [0,1] but f' is not polynomial time computable. (A function m is a <u>modulus</u> <u>of</u> <u>absolute</u> <u>continuity</u> of f if for all $n \geq 1$ and for all finite collections of disjoint intervals $\{(a_i, b_i)\}_{i=1}^{k}$ in [0,1],

$$\sum_{i=1}^{k} |f(b_i) - f(a_i)| \leq 2^{-n}$$

whenever

$$\sum_{i=1}^{k} (b_i - a_i) \leq 2^{-m(n)}.)$$

From Theorem 3.9, if a function $f \in P_{C[0,1]}$ is analytic on [0,1], then every coefficient of its power series at, say,

36

1/2, is polynomial time computable. Are the coefficients, as a sequence of real numbers, polynomial time computable? That is, is the sequence $\{f^{(n)}(1/2)\}_{n=0}^{\infty}$ polynomial time computable in the sense that there is a polynomial time TM M which takes two inputs $n \in N$ and $k \in N$ and outputs a dyadic rational d such that $|d - f^{(n)}(1/2)| \leq 2^{-k}$? From Cauchy's integral formula, we can reduce this question to the question of the complexity of a sequence of integrals, and get the following result.

<u>Corollary 3.11.</u> Let $f \in P_{C[0,1]}$ be analytic on $[0,1]$. Then the sequence $\{f^{(n)}(1/2)\}_{n=0}^{\infty}$ is a polynomial time computable sequence if $P = \#P$.

It is not known whether the converse of Corollary 3.11 holds.

3.6 <u>Ordinary Differential Equations</u>
The basic question to be considered here is the following. Let $f(x,y)$ be a polynomial time computable function defined on $[0,1] \times [-1,1]$, what is the complexity of the function y of the following ordinary differential equation (E): $y'(x) = f(x,y(x))$, $y(0) = 0$? In recursive analysis, the following results have been known.

(1) If the function f is computable and the equation (E) has a unique solution y, then y is also computable [67].

(2) There exists a function $f(x,y)$ computable on the rectangle $[0,1] \times [-1,1]$ but no solution of (E) is computable on any interval $[0,\delta]$, $\delta > 0$ [2,67].

37

(3) For any recursive real number $a \in (0,1)$, there exists a primitive recursive real function f on $[0,1] \times [-1,1]$ such that $y(x) = ax^2$ is the unique solution of (E) [56].

(4) Assume that f satisfies the Lipschitz condition (i.e., there is a constant $L > 0$ such that $|f(x,z_1) = f(x,z_2)| \leq L \cdot |z_1 - z_2|$ for all $x \in [0,1]$ and $z_1, z_2 \in [-1,1]$). Then, for any $n \geq 3$, the (unique) solution y of (E) is in $\mathcal{E}^{(n)}$, the nth level of the Grzegorczyk hierarchy [21], whenever $f \in \mathcal{E}^{(n)}$ [12].

The above result (2) can be extended to polynomial time computable functions.

Theorem 3.12 [43]. There exists a polynomial time computable function f on $[0,1] \times [-1,1]$ such that the equation (E) has no computable solution y on $[0,\delta]$ for any $\delta > 0$.

Furthermore, the result (3) above also has a polynomial time analog.

Theorem 3.13 [43]. For any recursive function ϕ, there is a polynomial time computable real function f on $[0,1] \times [-1,1]$ such that the time complexity of the unique solution y to the equation (E) is not bounded by ϕ.

From the above results, it appears that the most interesting case is when the function f satisfies the linear Lipschitz condition. Is the solution y to (E) polynomial time computable, if f is polynomial time computable and satisfies the Lipschitz condition? we have the following partial results:

38

(1)   If f is polynomial time computable and satisfies the Lipschitz condition, then y is polynomial space computable. (By a simple analysis of Euler's method; see [28].)

(2)   If we relax the Lipschitz condition to a weaker local Lipschitz condition, then the above question has an affirmative answer iff P = PSPACE.

More precisely, we say a real function f on $[0,1] \times [-1,1]$ satisfies the right Lipschitz condition on a set $A \subseteq$ $[0,1] \times [-1,1]$ if there exists a constant $L > 0$ such that for all $x \in [0,1]$ and $z_1, z_2 \in [-1,1]$, if $z_1 < z_2$ and the line segment connecting (x, z_1) and (x, z_2) lies entirely inside A, then $f(x, z_2) - f(x, z_1) \leq L \cdot (z_2 - z_1)$. Then we have the following result.

<u>Theorem 3.14</u> [43]. The following statements are equivalent.

(a)   Let f be a polynomial time computable function on $[0,1] \times [-1,1]$ such that the equation (E) with respect to f has a unique solution y on $[0,1]$. Assume that there is a set $A \subseteq [0,1] \times [-1,1]$, and a polynomial function p, such that

   (i)   f satisfies the right Lipschitz condition on A, and

   (ii)   for each $k \geq 1$, $\{(x,z) : 0 \leq x \leq 1 - 2^{-k},$ $|z - y(x)| \leq 2^{-p(k)}\} \subseteq A.$
Then y is polynomial time computable.

(b)   P = PSPACE.

The proof technique of direction (a) => (b) of Theorem 3.14 is to construct a function f such that its solution y encodes the well known PSPACE-complete problem QBF (the quantified Boolean formula problem; see [18]). For each quantified Boolean formula, there is a self-reducing tree for it [55, 40]. For each self-reducing tree T, a function f_T is constructed in such a way that the computation of the solution y_T at $x + \epsilon$ from the solution $y_T(x)$ is similar to the traversal of the self-reducing tree T in an alpha-beta pruning algorithm. Therefore, the solution $y_T(x + \epsilon)$ encodes all the information contained in $y_T(x)$ plus the traversal of some new nodes in the self-reducing tree T. The final value $y_T(1)$ then encodes the complete tree T. The required function f then can be constructed as the combination of all f_T's. Since QBF is a PSPACE-complete problem, the solution y of f is polynomial time computable iff P = PSPACE.

The original question of the complexity of the solution y of (E), with f polynomial time computable and satisfying the two-sided, global Lipschitz condition, remains an interesting open question.

4. STRUCTURE OF REAL NUMBERS AND REAL FUNCTIONS

It was shown in Section 3.3 that the maximum values of polynomial time computable functions are real numbers with NP left cuts. However, we did not find an exact classification of the complexity of NP left cuts. More precisely, we know that $P = NP \Rightarrow P_R = NP_R \Rightarrow P_1 = NP_1$ but do not know whether $P_1 = $

$NP_1 \Rightarrow P_R = NP_R$ or $P_R = NP_R \Rightarrow P = NP$. In this section, we discuss in more detail the realtionship between the complexity and the structural properties of left cuts and give a partial classification of NP left cuts into the recently constructed high and low hierarchies in NP [77,45]. Furthermore, in Section 4.3, we investigate the relative complexity of real numbers and its relation to the structure of computable real functions.

4.1 Standard Left Cuts and P-Selective Sets

The structure of recursively enumerable (r.e.) standard left cuts has been carefully studies by Soare [83,84]. In particular, he used standard left cuts as a tool to derive new results in recursion theory. Here we only summarize the most important results about the completeness of the standard left cuts.

An important structureal property of a standard left cut L (defined in Section 2.1) is that $(\forall s, t \in \{0,1\}^*)[[s \leq t$ and $t \in L]$ implies $s \in L]$. This structural property is useful in proving incompleteness results of standard left cuts.

We first define semirecursive sets and p-selective sets. Semirecursive sets were introduced by Jockusch [30] to distinguish reducibilities on r.e. sets.

Definition 4.1. A set $A \subseteq \{0,1\}^*$ is called <u>semirecursive</u> if there is a recursive function $\phi : \{0,1\}^* \times \{0,1\}^* \rightarrow \{0,1\}^*$ such that $(\forall s, t \in \{0,1\}^*)[\phi(s,t) \in \{s,t\}$, and $[[s \in A$ or $t \in A]$ implies $\phi(s,t) \in A]]$. The function ϕ is called a <u>selector</u> for A.

41

The polynomial time analog of semirecursive sets is called p-selective sets. Selman [78] used p-selective sets to distinguish polynomial time reducibilities.

Definition 4.2. A set $A \subseteq \{0,1\}^*$ is called p-selective if A is semirecursive and A has a polynomial time computable selector.

It is easily seen that a standard left cut is p-selective. Therefore, many results about semirecursive and p-selective sets obtained by Jockusch [30] and Selman [78] hold for standard left cuts too. In particular, the following results about r.e. standard left cuts are immediate [84,79].

(1) No r.e. standard left cut can be $\leq_{ptt}$-complete, where $\leq_{ptt}$ is the positive truth-table reducibility [74].

(2) There exists an r.e. standard left cut which is $\leq_{tt}$-complete but not $\leq_{ptt}$-complete.

Another interesting recursion-theoretic property of r.e. standard left cuts is the following: An r.e. set $A \subseteq N$ is called pseudocreative if (1) for any r.e. set $B \subseteq \overline{A}$, there is an infinite r.e. set $C \subseteq \overline{A} - B$, and (2) A is not creative (i.e., A is not $\leq_m$-complete) [74]. It is shown in Ko [36] that an r.e. standard left cut is either recursive or pseudocreative.

One of the ideas in the proofs of the above results is to relate the standard left cut L_x of $x \in [0,1]$ to the binary expansion B_x of x, where $B_x = \{0^n : $ the nth bit of the binary expansion of x is 1$\}$. More precisely, we show that

(1) $L_x \leq^P_{ptt} B_x$ and (2) $B_x \leq_{tt} L_x$ and $B_x \leq^P_T L_x$ [79,39]. These relations allow us to construct, say, $\leq_{tt}$-complete left cuts easily. However, these results do not hold for general left cuts, and therefore we need to find a more general structural property than p-selectivity for general left cuts.

4.2 General Left Cuts and Weakly P-Selective Sets

A general left cut L has the property that $(\forall s, t \in \{0,1\}*)$ $[[\ell th(s) = \ell th(t),\ s \leq t\ \text{and}\ t \in L]\ \text{implies}\ s \in L]$. In other words, there is a p-selector ϕ which, for any two given strings s and t of the same length, selects the smaller one. This suggests the following definition of a weakly p-selective set as a generalization of that of a p-selective set.

<u>Definition 4.3</u> [40,45]. A set $A \subseteq \{0,1\}*$ is called <u>weakly p-selective</u> if there is a polynomial time computable function ϕ, and a polynomial function p such that for every $n \in N$, the set $\{s \in \{0,1\}* : \ell th(s) \leq n\}$ can be decomposed into at most $p(n)$ many pairwisely disjoint subsets $B_1, \ldots, B_m$, $m \leq p(n)$, and

(1) $(\forall i, j \leq m,\ i \neq j)(\forall s \in B_i)(\forall t \in B_j)[\phi(s,t) = \#]$,
and

(2) $(\forall i \leq m)(\forall s, t \in B_i)[\phi(s,t) \in \{s,t\}\ \text{and}\ [[s \in A\ \text{or}\ t \in A]\ \text{implies}\ \phi(s,t) \in A]]$.

It is obvious that both p-selective sets and left cuts of
real numbers are weakly p-selective.

In the recent investigation of the structure of NP sets,
some interesting results on the relationship between the density
of a set and its completeness in NP have been obtained.
Berman [5] first proved that a tally set (i.e., a set of strings
over a single-letter alphabet) cannot be $\leq_m^P$-complete for NP
unless P = NP. Fortune [16] showed that a sparse set cannot
be $\leq_m^P$-complete for co-NP unless P = NP. (A set A is
sparse if there is a polynomial function p such that for any
$n \in N$, the number of strings in A which are of lengths $\leq n$
is $\leq p(n)$.) Mahaney [54] showed that a sparse set cannot be
$\leq_m^P$-complete for NP unless P = NP. The proofs of these
results use the self-reducibility property of the well known
NP-complete problem SATISFIABILITY [55,40].

Using an "initial segment" characterization of weakly p-
selective sets, we can show that the property of weak p-
selectivity is, similar to sparseness, incompatible with the
self-reducibility property. Namely, a weakly p-selective set
(and hence a left cut) cannot be $\leq_m^P$-complete for NP unless
P = NP, and it cannot be $\leq_m^P$-complete for PSPACE unless
P = PSPACE [36,40].

Another similar result on the incompatibility between NP-
completeness and sparseness is Karp and Lipton [33] and
Sipser's result that a set having polynomial size circuits
cannot be $\leq_T^P$-complete for NP unless the polynomial time
hierarchy of Meyer-Stockmeyer collapses to the second level Σ_2^P.

(For the definitions of circuit-size complexity and the polynomial time hierarchy, the reader is referred to Karp and Lipton [33] and Stockmeyer [88].) A consequence of Karp, Lipton, and Sipser's result is that tally sets, sparse sets, co-sparse sets, and sets computable by polynomial time probabilistic TM's with one-sided errors [19,4] cannot be $\leq_T^P$-complete for NP unless the polynomial time hierarchy collapses to Σ_2^P.

Using the initial segment characterization of weakly p-selective sets, Ko [40] and Selman [79] showed that weakly p-selective sets have polynomial size circuits. Therefore, a weakly p-selective set (and hence a left cut) cannot be $\leq_T^P$-complete for NP unless the polynomial time hierarchy collapses to Σ_2^P.

Using the initial segment characterization of weakly p-selective sets, Ko [40] and Selman [79] showed that weakly p-selective sets have polynomial size circuits. Therefore, a weakly p-selective set (and hence a left cut) cannot be $\leq_T^P$-complete for NP unless the polynomial time hierarchy collapses to Σ_2^P.

A high and a low hierarchy in NP as an analog of the high and low hierarchy in the degree theory of r.e. sets has been defined and proved useful in classifying the structural properties of sets in NP [77,45]. In particular, NP-complete sets (with respect to various types of polynomial time reducibilities) are known to be in the high hierarchy, and a set in the low hierarchy cannot be NP-complete unless the polynomial time hierarchy collapses. Berman, Fortune, Mahaney, and Karp, Lipton and Sipser's results suggest that sparse sets and tally sets in NP are in the low hierarchy. Indeed, Ko and Schöning [45] proved that sets having polynomial size circuits are in L_3^P, the third level of the low hierarchy, and that sparse sets, tally sets and weakly p-selective sets are in L_2^P, the second level of the low hierarchy. Thus we have that an NP left cut in in L_2^P. This is the best classification of NP left cuts since it is known that $EXP \neq NEXP$ implies that there is an NP left cut which is not in $L_1^P = NP \cap co\text{-}NP$.

An immediate consequence of the above results is a generalization of Karp, Lipton, and Sipser's result: A left cut L cannot be $\leq_T^{snp}$-complete in NP unless the polynomial time hierarchy collapses to Σ_2^P, where $\leq_T^{snp}$ is the strong non-deterministic polynomial time Turing reducibility [53] which is known to be weaker than $\leq_T^P$ (i.e., $A \leq_T^P B$ implies $A \leq_T^{snp} B$).

The major question about the complexity of NP left cuts remains open: Is there a characterization of the complexity of NP left cuts in terms of the complexity bounded classes of discrete complexity theory?

4.3 Relative Complexity of Real Numbers

The concept of reducibility has been useful in classifying the degrees of unsolvability of nonrecursive problems in recursion theory [74] and in classifying the degrees of complexity of subrecursive problems in complexity theory [52]. In this section we apply the concept of reducibility to real numbers to gain some insight into the structure of reducibilities and their relation to some analytical properties of real functions.

46

Two classes of reducibilities are proposed. First, a real function is regarded as a reduction function, and a class of real functions satisfying some computational or analytical properties forms a certain kind of reducibility.

Definition 4.4 [42]. Let F be a class of real functions. We say a real number x is F-reducible to a real number y, and write x $\leq_F$ y, if there is a function f ∈ F such that f(y) = x.

Intuitively, if we regard a Cauchy sequence representation of a real number as a type 1 function, then a real function is a type 2 function and, naturally, can be used as a reduction function. In other words, if f(y) = x and f is computable, then for any φ ∈ CS(y), a function ψ ∈ CS(x) is uniquely determined by the machine which computes f and the oracle φ. Therefore we say f reduces x to y.

Many interesting reducibilities can easily be defined from Definition 4.4 by letting F be a subclass of the class of computable real functions with some interesting properties. For example,

$\leq_{RF}$: reducibility by recursive real functions,

$\leq_{IRF}$: reducibility by increasing, recursive real functions,

$\leq_{DRF}$: reducibility by differentiable, recursive real functions,

$\leq_{PF}$: reducibility by polynomial time computable functions,

$\leq_{IPF}$: reducibility by increasing, polynomial time
            computable functions,

$\leq_{NPF}$: reducibility by NP real functions.

Next we define the second class of reducibilities which is a generalization of the machine-based reducibilities in recursion theory and discrete complexity theory [74,52].

Definition 4.5. Let $\leq_r$ be one of the following reducibilities: $\leq_T$, $\leq_{tt}$, and $\leq_m$. We say a real number x is $\leq_r^R$-reducible to a real number y, and write $x \leq_r^R y$, if there is a reduction algorithm A of type r such that for any set $L \in LC(y)$, there is a set $L' \in LC(x)$ such that $L' \leq_r L$ via A.

By a reduction algorithm A of type r, we mean a Turing machine if $r = T$, a truth-table generator and evaluator if $r = tt$, and a computable many-one function if $r = m$.

Polynomial time reducibilities on real numbers, such as $\leq_T^{P,R}$, $\leq_m^{P,R}$, and $\leq_T^{NP,R}$, can be similarly defined.

We note that Definition 4.5 is a natural extension of the reducibilities in recursion theory to the objects which have more than one representation. For example, we can show that if $x \leq_m^R y$ and y is recursive, then x is recursive from the above definition of $\leq_m^R$ easily. In the proof of this result, it is important to require a fixed reduction function ϕ for all left cuts L of y and the corresponding L' in $LC(x)$, because we need to have a unique algorithm to determine the membership problem in $L' \in LC(x)$ from that in a given $L \in LC(y)$.

48

In the following we discuss the characterization of some reducibilities in the first class, which are defined by some analytical properties as well as some complexity-theoretic properties of real functions, by the reducibilities of the second class, which are defined by purely complexity-theoretic properties. Thus some connections between the complexity-theoretic properties and the analytical properties are established. Our main results can be summarized as follows [42]. We treat a reducibility as a binary relation on real numbers.

$$\left.\begin{array}{c} \leq_{IRF} = \leq_m^R \\[2em] \leq_{DRF} \end{array}\right\} \subsetneq \leq_{RF} = \leq_{tt}^R \subsetneq \leq_T^R,$$

$$\leq_{IPF} = \leq_m^{P,R} \subsetneq \leq_{PF} = \leq_T^{P,R} \subseteq \leq_{NPF} = \leq_T^{NP,R}.$$

In particular, we have $\leq_{RF} = \leq_{tt}^R$ rather than $\leq_{RF} = \leq_T^R$. This is because a recursive real function f must have a recursive modulus function and therefore, when used as a reduction function, is nonadaptive, whereas $\leq_T^R$ is an adaptive reducibility. The result $\leq_{IRF} = \leq_m^R$ is also interesting because here the concept of monotonicity of a real function is shown to be equivalent to a purely recursion-theoretic concept of many-one reduction. This result becomes natural, however, if one compares the definition of the many-one reducibility with that of p-selective sets and weakly p-selective sets (see Sections 4.1 and 4.2). We sketch a proof for this result to give some flavor of the proof techniques used in [42].

First, if $f(y) = x$ and f is increasing, then for any dyadic rational number d, we can find effectively a dyadic rational number e such that $|f(e) - d| \leq 2^{-\ell th(d)}$, and the mapping $\phi(d) = e$ can be used as a many-one reduction function for $x \leq_m^R y$.

Conversely, assume that ϕ is a computable function such that for any set $L \in LC(y)$, ϕ reduces a set $L' \in LC(x)$ to L. Then, a monotonic increasing, computable function f with $f(y) = x$ may be (tentatively) defined as follows:

$f(z) = \lim_{n \to \infty} d_n$, where d_n is the greatest dyadic rational number of length $\leq n$ which satisfies $\phi(d_n) \leq z$.

To make sure that the limit of d_n exists, we check that if $z = y$ then $\lim d_n$ must exist and is equal to x. Since we want only $f(y) = x$, a "smoothening" technique can be used to make $f(y) = x$ and also make f to be well-defined and computable. To be more precise, we modify the definition of $f(z)$ as follows:

$f(z) = \lim_{n \to \infty} d_n'$, where

$$
d_n' = \begin{cases} d_n & \text{if } |d_n - d_{n-1}'| \leq 2^{-n} \\ d_{n-1}' + 2^{-n} & \text{if } d_n > d_{n-1}' + 2^{-n} \\ d_{n-1}' - 2^{-n} & \text{if } d_n < d_{n-1}' - 2^{-n}. \end{cases}
$$

50

It can be checked that this smoothening technique also ensures the monotonicity of the function f.

One of the interesting open questions here is to find a recursion-theoretic characterization of the reducibility $\leq_{DRF}$. Such a characterization would give us the first nontrivial relation between the concept of differentiation and some computaional concept.

It should be pointed out that the first class of reducibilities, i.e., reducibilities via real functions, provides abundant interesting reducibilities. For example, for each $k \geq 1$, let $\leq_{kDRF}$ denote the reducibility defined by recursive functions which are in $C^k[0,1]$. Then we have a potentially infinite hierarchy of reducibilities. It is an interesting question whether these reducibilities are useful in classifying the degrees of unsolvability of real numbers.

5. FUTURE DIRECTIONS

In the above three sections, we have introduced a complexity theory of numerical computation and reviewed some main issues in this theory. It seems that we have benefited much from the new concepts and techniques developed in discrete complexity theory, and have begun to discover some interesting connections between numerical and discrete computation. It should be clear, however, that many more questions and issues have been left untouched. In the following we discuss some of the most important ones.

(1) Extension of the theory. In our theory, we have only discussed the computational complexity of real functions and the
related operations. However, it appears that the concepts and
the proof techniques can also be applied to more general numerical constructs. In recursive analysis, the theory has been
successfully extended to recursive metric space and higher-
order functionals [11,46,59,60,76]. There seems to be a
straightforward formulation of the concept of computational
complexity in a recursive metric space, and questions on the
complexity of operations may be studied from a more general
viewpoint. This could be the beginning of a general theory of
numerical algorithms (cf. [90,89]).

(2) Analytical properties and complexity. The results we have
obtained so far in this direction are limited. Despite our
negative results about the tractability of the numerical operations, such as integration and differentiation, numerous
algorithms for these operations exist and continue to work
"efficiently." It is important to understand the constraints
on the real functions under which efficient algorithms exist.
Certain techniques used in the analysis of discrete algorithms
may be applicable here. More importantly, however, new techniques, evolved from both the areas of numerical analysis and
discrete complexity theory, have to be developed to deal with
the complex numerical constructs. One interesting example is
Miller's [58] study of the relationship between computational
complexity and numerical stability.

(3) Average-case complexity. Another explanation of the existence of numerous practical algorithms for the intractable numerical operations studied in Section 3 is that we have concentrated on the worst-case complexity and have been con-servative. It would be interesting to see that the average-case complexity of these algorithms is low. The study of average-case complexity in discrete complexity theory has not been as successful as that of worst-case complexity. One reason has been the difficulty of establishing a practical probability distribution of the problem instances (cf. [32]). This problem may find a solution in the complexity theory of numerical algo-rithms because the classical measure theory provides a well-founded setting for the problem. Smale [82], Shub and Smale [81], and Blum and Shub [6] recently demonstrated some tech-niques for average-case analysis of numerical algorithms.

(4) Numerical computation and discrete computation. In Section 4 we demonstrated that the high and low hierarchies are useful in classifying the degree of complexity of the left cut structure. It would be interesting to see more applications of discrete complexity theory to numerical problems. For example, can we apply the approximation algorithms for NP-hard combinatorial problems [18] to some numerical problems? On the other hand, some techniques developed in numerical analysis may be applied to some discrete problems. One example is the application of results in matrix theory to the problems in graph theory. A uniform complexity theory to deal with both numerical and discrete algorithms is desirable and may be

developed from these applications. Traub, Wasilkowski and Woźniakowski [89] have made a first step toward such a theory.

NOTES

1. There are at least two different approaches in recursive analysis. The first approach studies the computability problem of real functions in the context of classical real analysis. For instance, a recursive real function is defined to be a recursive operator on the set of all Cauchy sequences that converge to some real numbers. Some earlier work in this approach include Grzegorczyk [22,23,24], Lacombe [48,49,50], and Mostowski [61,62]. The second approach is more constructive and studies only recursive objects in real analysis. In this theory, a recursive real function is defined to be a recursive operator on the set of all recursive functions which compute recursive real numbers. The main contributors in this approach include Moschovakis [59,60], Goodstein [20], Šanin [76], Ceitin [11], and Aberth [1,3]. The complexity theory to be discussed in this theory is based on the first approach. In the subsequent discussions of results in recursive analysis we refer only to those from the first approach.

2. A recursive real function which is not strictly monotone may have infinitely many roots, with none of them recursive. This fact follows immediately from Specker's [86] theorem that there exists a recursive real function which has infinitely many maximum points but none of them is recursive. This observation was pointed out to the author by Professors M. Pour-El and W.Q. Huang.

ACKNOWLEDGMENTS
The author thanks Professor M. Pour-El and referees for their valuable comments. The criticism of one of the referees has greatly influenced the style of the final version. The author also thanks Professor R.V. Book for his encouragement. The research was supported in part by the National Science Foundation under Grants Nos. MCS81-03479 and MCS82-15544.

BIBLIOGRAPHY

[1] Aberth, O., Analysis in the computable number field. Journal of the Association for Computing Machinery 15 (1968), 275-299.

[2] Aberth, O., The failure in computable analysis of a classical existence theorem for differential equations. Proceedings of the American Mathematical Society 30(1971), 151-156.

[3] Aberth, O., Computable analysis. New York: McGraw-Hill (1980).

[4] Adleman, L., Two theorems on random polynomial time. Proceedings of the 19th IEEE Symposium on Foundations of Computer Science (1978), 75-83.

[5] Berman, P., Relationship between density and deterministic complexity of NP-complete languages. Proceedings of the 5th International Colloquium on Automata, Languages, and Programming, Lecture Notes in Computer Science 62(1978), 63-71.

[6] Blum, L. and Shub, M., Evaluating rational functions: infinite precision is finite cost and tractable on average. Proceedings of the 25th IEEE Symposium on Foundations of Computer Science (1984), 261-267.

[7] Blum, M., A machine-independent theory of the complexity of recursive functions. Journal of the Association for Computing Machinery 14(1967), 322-366.

[8] Book, R.V., Tally languages and complexity classes. Information and Control 26(1974), 186-193.

[9] Borodin, A.B., Computational complexity and the existence of complexity gaps. Journal of the Association for Computing Machinery 19(1972), 158-174.

[10] Borodin, A. and Munro, I., The computational complexity of algebraic and numeric problems. New York: American Elsevier (1975).

[11] Ceitin, G.S., Algorithmic operators in constructive metric spaces. American Mathematical Society Translations (English Translation) 64(1967), 1-80.

[12] Cleave, J., The primitive recursive analysis of ordinary differential equations and the complexity of their solutions. Journal of Computer and System Sciences 3(1969), 447-455.

[13] Cobham, A., The intrinsic computational difficulty of functions. Proceedings of the International Congress for Logic, Methodology and Philosophy of Science (Y. Bar-Hillel, editor), Amsterdam: North-Holland (1964), 24-30.

[14] Constable, R.L., Type two computational complexity. Proceedings of the 5th ACM Symposium on Theory of Computing (1973), 108-121.

[15] Cook, S.A., The complexity of theorem-proving procedures. Proceedings of the 3rd ACM Symposium on Theory of Computing (1971), 151-158.

[16] Fortune, S., A note on sparse complete sets. SIAM Journal on Computing 8(1979), 431-433.

[17] Friedman, H., On the computational complexity of maximization and integration. Advances in Mathematics 53(1984), 80-98.

[18] Garey, M.R. and Johnson, D.S., Computers and intractability. San Francisco: Freeman (1979).

[19] Gill, J., Computational complexity of probabilistic Turing machines. SIAM Journal on Computing 6(1977), 675-695.

[20] Goodstein, R.L., Recursive analysis. Amsterdam: North-Holland (1961).

[21] Grzegorczyk, A., Some classes of recursive functions. Rozprawy Matematyczne 4(1953), 1-46.

[22] Grzegorczyk, A., Computable functionals. Fundamenta Mathematicae 42(1955), 168-202.

[23] Grzegorczyk, A., On the definitions of computable real continuous functions. Fundamenta Mathematicae 44(1957), 61-71.

[24] Grzegorczyk, A., Some approaches to constructive analysis. Constructivity in mathematics (A. Heyting, editor), Amsterdam: North-Holland (1959), 43-61.

[25] Hartmanis, J. and Stearns, R.E., On the computational complexity of algorithms. Transactions of the American Mathematical Society 117(1965), 285-306.

[26] Hartmanis, J., Lewis, P.M., II, and Stearns, R.E., Hierarchies of memory limited computations. Proceedings of the 6th IEEE Symposium on Switching Circuit Theory and Logical Design (1965), 179-190.

[27] Hartmanis, J., Feasible computations and provable complexity properties. Philadelphia: SIAM (1978).

[28] Henrici, P., Discrete variable methods in ordinary differential equations, Ch. 1. New York: Wiley and Sons (1962).

[29] Henrici, P., Applied and computational complex analysis, Vol. 1. New York: Wiley-Interscience (1974).

[30] Jockusch, C., Jr., Semirecursive sets and positive reducibility. Transactions of the American Mathematical Society 137(1968), 420-436.

[31] Karp, R.M., Reducibility among combinatorial problems. Complexity of computer computations (R.E. Miller and J.W. Thatcher, editors), New York: Plenum Press (1972), 85-103.

[32] Karp, R.M., The probabilistic analysis of some combinatorial search algorithms. Algorithms and complexity (J.F. Traub, editor), New York: Academic Press (1976), 1-19.

[33] Karp, R.M. and Lipton, R., Some connections between nonuniform and uniform complexity classes. Proceedings of the 12th ACM Symposium on Theory of Computing (1980), 302-309.

[34] Knuth, D., The art of computer programming, Vol. 2, Seminumerical algorithms. Reading, Mass.: Addison-Wesley (1981).

[35] Ko, K., Continuous optimization problems and a polynomial hierarchy of real functions. Journal of Complexity 1 (1985), to appear.

[36] Ko, K., The maximum value problem and NP real numbers. Journal of Computer and System Sciences 24(1982), 15-35.

[37] Ko, K., Some negative results on the computational complexity of total variation and differentiation. Information and Control 53(1982), 21-31.

[38] Ko, K., Approximation to measurable functions and its relation to probabilistic computation. Annals of Pure and Applied Logic 30(1986), to appear.

[39] Ko, K., On the definitions of some complexity classes of real numbers. Mathematical Systems Theory 16(1983), 95-109.

[40] Ko, K., On self-reducibility and weak p-selectivity. Journal of Computer and System Sciences 26(1983), 209-221.

[41] Ko, K., On the computational complexity of differentiation. Technical Report #UH-CS-83-2, Department of Computer Science, University of Houston, Houston, Texas (1983).

[42] Ko, K., Reducibilities on real numbers. Theoretical Computer Science 31(1984), 101-123.

[43] Ko, K., On the computational complexity of ordinary differential equations. Information and Control 58(1983), 157-194.

[44] Ko, K. and Friedman, H., Computational complexity of real functions. Thoeretical Computer Science 20(1982), 323-352.

[45] Ko, K. and Schöning, U., On circuit-size complexity and the low hierarchy in NP. SIAM Journal on Computing 14 (1985), 41-51.

[46] Kreisel, G. and Lacombe, D., Ensembles recursivement measurables et ensembles recursivement ouverts ou fermes. Comptes Rendus 245(1957), 1106-1109.

[47] Kreitz, C. and Weihrauch, K., Complexity theory on real numbers and functions. Lecture Notes in Computer Science 145(1982), 165-174.

[48] Lacombe, D., Extension de la notion de fonction recursive aux fonctions d'une ou plusiers variables reelles, and other notes. Comptes Rendus 240(1955), 2478-2480; 241(1955), 13-14, 151-153, 1250-1252.

[49] Lacombe, D., Les ensembles recursivement ouverts ou fermes et leurs applications a l'analyse recursive, and other notes. Comptes Rendus 244(1957), 838-840, 996-997; 245, 1040-1043.

[50] Lacombe, D., Quelques procedes de definition en topologie recursive. Constructivity in Mathematics (A. Heyting, editor), Amsterdam: North-Holland (1959), 129-158.

[51] Ladner, R.E., On the structure of polynomial time reducibility. Journal of the Association for Computing Machinery 22(1975), 155-171.

[52] Ladner, R.E., Lynch, N., and Selman, A.L., A comparison of polynomial time reducibilities. Theoretical Computer Science 1(1975), 103-123.

[53] Long, T.J., Strong nondeterministic polynomial time reducibilities. Theoretical Computer Science 21(1982), 1-25.

[54] Mahaney, S.R., Sparse complete sets in NP: solution of a conjecture by Berman and Hartmanis. Journal of Computer and System Sciences 25(1982), 130-143.

[55] Meyer, A.R. and Paterson, M.S., With what frequency are apparently intractable problems difficult? Technical Report MIT/LCS/TM-126, Laboratory for Computer Science, Massachusetts Institute of Technology (1979).

[56] Miller, W., Recursive function theory and numerical analysis. Journal of Computer and System Sciences 4(1970), 465-472.

[57] Miller, W., Toward abstract numerical analysis. Journal of the Association for Computing Machinery 20(1973), 399-408.

[58] Miller, W., Computational complexity and numerical stability. SIAM Journal on Computing 4(1975), 97-107.

[59] Moschovakis, Y., Notation systems and recursive ordered fields. Compositio Mathematica 17(1964), 40-71.

[60] Moschovakis, Y., Recursive metric spaces. Fundamenta Mathematicae 55(1964), 215-238.

[61] Mostowski, A., On computable sequences. Fundamenta Mathematicae 44(1957), 37-51.

[62] Mostowski, A., On various degrees of constructivism. Constructivity in Mathematics (A. Heyting, editor), Amsterdam: North-Holland (1959), 178-194.

[63] Myhill, J., A recursive function defined on a compact interval and having a continuous derivative that is not recursive. Michigan Mathematics Journal 18(1971), 97-98.

[64] Péter, R., Rekursive Funktionen. Budapest: Akadémiai Kiadó (1951).

[65] Pinkert, J.R., An exact method for finding the roots of a complex polynomial. ACM Transactions on Mathematical Software 2(1976), 351-363.

[66] Pour-El, M.B. and Richards, I., Differentiability properties of computable functions--a summary. Acta Cybernetica 4(1978), 123-125.

[67] Pour-El, M.B. and Richards, I., A computable ordinary differential equation which possesses no computable solution. Annals of Mathematical Logic 17(1979), 61-90.

[68] Pour-El, M.B. and Richards, I., The wave equation with
computable initial data such that its unique solution is
not computable. Advances in Mathematics 39(1981), 215-239.

[69] Pour-El, M.B. and Richards, I., Computability and noncomputability in classical analysis. Transactions of the
American Mathematical Society 275(1983), 539-560.

[70] Pour-El, M.B. and Richards, I., Noncomputability in
analysis and physics: a complete determination of the
class of noncomputable linear operators. Advances in
Mathematics 48(1983), 44-74.

[71] Rabin, M.O., Probabilistic algorithms. Algorithms and
Complexity (J.F. Traub, editor), New York: Academic Press
(1976), 21-39.

[72] Rice, H.G., Recursive real numbers. Proceedings of the
American Mathematical Society 5(1954), 784-791.

[73] Robinson, R.M., Review of Péter: Rekursive funktionen.
Journal of Symbolic Logic 16(1951), 280-282.

[74] Rogers, H., Jr., Theory of recursive functions and effective computability. New York: McGraw-Hill (1967).

[75] Rosenbloom, P.C., An elementary constructive proof of the
fundamental theorem of algebra. American Mathematical
Monthly 52(1945), 562-570.

[76] Šanin, N.A., Constructive real numbers and function
spaces (English translation, E. Mendelson). Providence,
R.I.: American Mathematical Society (1968).

[77] Schöning, U., A high and a low hierarchy within NP.
Journal of Computer and System Sciences 27(1983), 14-28.

[78] Selman, A.L., P-selective sets, tally languages and the
behavior of polynomial time reducibilities on NP. Mathematical Systems Theory 13(1979), 55-65.

[79] Selman, A.L., Some observations on NP real numbers and
p-selective sets. Journal of Computer and System Sciences
23(1981), 326-332.

[80] Shepherdson, J.C., On the definition of computable function
of a real variable. Zeitschrift für Mathematische Logik
und Grundlagen der Mathematik 22(1976), 391-402.

[81] Shub, M. and Smale, S., Computational complexity on the
geometry of polynomials and a theory of cost: Part I.
Center for Pure and Applied Mathematics Report, University
of California, Berkeley (1982).

[82] Smale, S., The fundamental theory of algebra and complexity theory. Bulletin of the American Mathematical Society 4(1981), 1-36.

[83] Soare, R.I., Cohesive sets and recursively enumerable Dedekind cuts. Pacific Journal of Mathematics 31(1969), 215-231.

[84] Soare, R.I., Recursion theory and Dedekind cuts. Transactions of the American Mathematical Society 140(1969), 271-294.

[85] Specker, E., Nich konstruktive beweisbare Satze der Analysis. Journal of Symbolic Logic 14(1949), 145-158.

[86] Specker, E., Der satz vom maximum in der rekursiven analysis. Constructivity in Mathematics (A. Heyting, editor), Amsterdam: North-Holland (1959), 254-265.

[87] Specker, E., The fundamental theorem of algebra in recursive analysis. Proceedings of the Symposium on Constructive Aspects of the Fundamental Theorem of Algebra, (B. Dejon and P. Henrici, editors), New York: Wiley-Interscience (1969), 321-329.

[88] Stockmeyer, L.J., The polynomial-time hierarchy. Theoretical Computer Science 3(1977), 1-22.

[89] Traub, J.F., Wasilkowski, G.W., and Woźniakowski, H., Information, uncertainty, complexity. Reading, Mass.: Addison-Wesley (1983).

[90] Traub, J.F. and Woźniakowski, H., A general theory of optimal algorithms. New York: Academic Press (1980).

[91] Turing, A.M., On computable numbers, with an application to the Entscheidungs problem. Proceedings of the London Mathematical Society 42(1936), 230-265.

[92] Valiant, L.G., The complexity of computing the permanent. Theoretical Computer Science 8(1979), 189-201.

[93] Valiant, L.G., The complexity of enumeration and reliability problems. SIAM Journal on Computing 8(1979), 410-421.

[94] Weihrauch, K. and Kreitz, C., Representations of the real numbers and of the open subsets of the set of real numbers. Informatik Berichte 43(1984), Fern Universität, Hagen, West Germany.

[95] Wilf, H.S., A global bisection algorithm for computing the zeros of polynomials in the complex plane. Journal of the Association for Computing Machinery 25(1978), 415-420.

[96] Winograd, S., Some remarks on proof techniques in analytic complexity. Analytic Computational Complexity (J.F. Traub, editor), New York: Academic Press (1976), 5-14.

[97] Yao, A.C., Probabilistic computations: toward a unified measure of complexity. Proceedings of the 18th IEEE Symposium on Foundations of Computer Science (1977), 222-227.

Ker-I Ko
Department of Computer Science
University of Houston
Houston, Texas 77004, U.S.A.

STEPHEN R MAHANEY
Sparse sets and reducibilities

1. INTRODUCTION

Recent work has examined the consequences of the existence of
reductions from complete sets in NP, PTAPE and other
complexity classes to sparse sets. The existence of such
reductions is equivalent to those complete sets having tractable complexity in powerful computational models; for example,
small Boolean circuit complexity. If NP (or PTAPE)-
complete sets do not have deterministic, polynomial-time
algorithms on Turing machines, then small circuit complexity
is an attractive alternative.

However, several results show that from such reductions of
complete sets to sparse sets, we can construct efficient
algorithms for these complexity classes or bounds on the power
of time or tape as resources. As examples, if NP-complete
sets are polynomial, many-one reducible to sparse sets then
P = NP; and, if PTAPE-complete sets are polynomial, Turing
reducible to sparse sets, then PTAPE is in the polynomial
time hierarchy. The algorithms are derived from combining
sparseness with structural properties of complete sets (such
as self-reducibility of NP-complete sets or the alternating
games of PTAPE-complete sets).

This paper surveys recent results in this area: sparseness and tractability in circuits, proof techniques related to many-one reductions to sparse sets, and different techniques for Turing reductions. We begin by placing this work in the larger context of computational complexity.

Understanding the relationships of time, tape, and nondeterminism as computational resources has dominated computational complexity for approximately two decades. The relationships among the classes P, NP and PTAPE typify these questions at a tractable level of computation. (These denote, respectively, recognition by computations bounded by the resources of deterministic polynomial time, nondeterministic polynomial time, and polynomial space.) The containments $P \subseteq NP \subseteq PTAPE$ are well known. Establishing the equalities or inequalities among these classes is central to determining the relative values of various resources for computation.

The principal tools for studying these classes are their complete sets; consider NP which is the class of sets of the form

$$A = \{x : \exists w \ (|w| \le q(|x|) \ \text{and} \ P(x,w))\},$$

where $q(\ )$ is a polynomial and $P(\ ,\ )$ is some polynomial time predicate. We think of w as the "witness" to x's membership in A. Then the NP-complete sets are defined to be sets C in NP such that every set in NP is efficiently reducible to C [8,24]. (Similar remarks apply to PTAPE and other resource bounded classes [19].) If any NP-complete set is in P, then P = NP; thus it suffices to characterize the resource requirements of any NP-complete set. However, the best known algorithms for complete sets in NP require exponential time.

Research on these questions has fallen into three broad categories:

1. What sets are NP-complete? The first is due to Cook:

SAT = {F a Boolean formula : there is a satisfying
          assignment for F}

was the first NP-complete set found [8] and it was notable for its natural combinatorial structure. Following quickly came other problems from graph theory and optimization [24], such as

HAM = {G an undirected graph : G has a Hamiltonian
          circuit}.

At the present, well over three hundred NP-complete problems are known [12] and there are hundreds of variations on these problems that remain NP-complete. The value of characterizing problems as NP-complete is in knowing that either no efficient algorithms will exist (P ≠ NP), or no efficient algorithm will be found until P = NP is proved. Each new NP-complete set underscores the importance of the P =? NP question. However, this variety of sets does not appear to provide insights to solve the P = NP question.

2. Finding approximations for problems that need solving. The complete problems include many with obvious applications. The TSP, or Traveling Salesman Problem, is a rough model of how to best route a pen plotter or a delivery van; the Bin Packing Problem models how to pack files onto the smallest number of disk memories; etc. An extensive literature deals with approximate solutions: In polynomial time can a solution ("approximate witness") be found that is guaranteed to be close to the optimal solution [12]? A typical result is: using a first-fit, decreasing heuristic for Bin Packing gives a solution that uses at most $4 + 11/9*OPT$, where OPT is the best possible solution [22]. Approximation results tend to be problem specific heuristics: the techniques that apply to Bin Packing do not transfer to TSP; small changes in the problem can preserve completeness (e.g., TSP on graphs with Triangle Inequality) but may permit better heuristics.

Approximations tend to be unrelated to the defining properties of NP-complete sets. First, it is not at all clear that every set in NP will have approximations. But what about the relation of basic defining properties of NP-completeness to approximate solutions. For example, if two sets A and B are NP-complete, the reductions of A to B will readily preserve witnesses for elements of A and B [43,5]. But, if A and B have approximations, it is generally not the case that reductions of A to B will preserve approximate solutions.

66

3.   Determine structural properties of P,   NP, PTAPE, etc.
What are the relationships among complete sets? Are there non-
complete sets? Even if P ≠ NP, can we solve these problems
efficiently by using small circuits or other means not available
to ordinary programs? For example, given the variety of known
NP-complete sets, it is perhaps surprising that all those sets
are equivalent under strong definitions of isomorphism [5].

This paper will address the structural question of whether
complete sets can be sparse (i.e., have considerable restrictions on the number of elements in the set, see below for
definition). The results examined here will show that reducibilities to sparse sets are sufficient to prove equalities
among certain resource bounded classes. (The precise statements of results depend on types of reductions.) Moreover,
reductions to sparse sets correspond naturally to solvability
by families of small circuits. Thus, if these classes P,   NP,
PTAPE are distinct, we are not able to efficiently solve NP-
and PTAPE-complete problems even with considerably stronger
models of computation that permit using polynomial table lookup
(a subclass of polynomial size circuits).

A specific example will clarify this argument. If an NP-
complete set, say SAT, is polynomial, many-one reducible to a
sparse set, then SAT is solvable by polynomial table lookup
(see Section 4 for details). This can be viewed as tractability for SAT in a non-uniform computational model. However,
the same hypothesis, that SAT is polynomial, many-one
reducible to a sparse set implies that SAT is in P, i.e.,

SAT is tractable in the ordinary sense of fast algorithms. Thus, for the NP-complete sets, if $P \neq NP$ they cannot be tractable in algorithms nor in these polynomial table lookup models.

But, note that polynomial table lookup methods are a stronger model of computation than polynomial time; for example, a tally set might encode an r.e. complete set. However, our results establish that this model is not stronger than polynomial time, when we apply it to NP-complete sets.

Although we indicate our prime motivation for studying sparse sets is based in computational questions, the structure and relations among computable sets is interesting in its own right. Even if $P \neq NP$ were established, it would be interesting to know if there are sparse sets in NP-P or whether sparseness implies that a set cannot be NP-complete.

In recursion theory we find a parallel analogy to these questions in the study of immune sets as an effort to find an r.e. degree that is not complete. From the definition of NP as sets

$$\{x : \exists w \ (|w| \leq q(|x|) \ \text{ and } \ P(x,w))\}$$

where $q(\ )$ is a polynomial and $P(\ , \ )$ is a polynomial time predicate we see the obvious analogy to r.e. sets given as

$$\{x : \exists t \ R(x,t)\}$$

where R(,) is a recursive predicate. The analogy continues
in the definitions of complete sets under polynomial and recursive reductions.

When Post [41] posed the problem of finding incomplete r.e.
sets, he observed that the known complete sets contained infinite r.e. sets in their complements. Thus, one attempt to
find incomplete sets was based on finding r.e. sets whose
complements are immune: i.e., contain no infinite r.e. set.
Informally, the complement is "thinned out." Although this and
subsequent attempts (with yet thinner hyperimmune and hyper-
hyperimmune sets) failed to solve Post's Problem, they provided
considerable information about the structure of r.e. degrees.

As we noted, the analogy to the P vs. NP problem is
inexact; nevertheless, under the assumption P ≠ NP, we have
already gained considerable knowledge about the structure of
sets in NP - P. However, we cannot promise that this work will
contribute directly to proving P ≠ NP.

2. BASIC DEFINITIONS; DENSITY AND SPARSENESS OF SETS

We will assume that the reader is familiar with basic definitions of deterministic and nondeterministic computation (with,
say, Turing machines as a model), with time and space bounded
computational complexity classes, and with oracle Turing
machines. This material can be found in [19] or [12].

We will use Σ to denote a finite alphabet containing at
least two symbols. We use Σ^* to denote the set of all
strings formed from Σ, and Σ^{*n} to denote the strings of Σ^*
of length up to and including n. The sets discussed here are

subsets of Σ^*; and functions are from strings to strings.
(An exception to the two symbol requirement is tally sets, when
Σ has one symbol.)

We will use P to denote sets recognized in polynomial time
by deterministic machines; NP for sets recognized in polynomial time by nondeterministic machines; co-NP for the
complements of sets in NP; and PTAPE for sets recognized in
polynomial tape (or space) by deterministic machines. Gener-
alizing the classes P and NP are sets in the polynomial
time hierarchy: Σ_k^P, Π_k^P, Δ_k^P [39,48]. Slightly less standard
notations are L and NL for sets recognized with tape
bounded by $\log(|\text{input}|)$ for computations, respectively, by
deterministic and nondeterministic machines. Finally, we use
EXPTIME, NEXPTIME, and EXPTAPE to denote classes with exponential resource bounds: for example, a set in EXPTIME is
accepted in $\text{TIME}[2^{cn}]$ for some $c > 0$.

Certain containment relations are known among these classes;
the results are based on straightforward simulations and can be
easily derived or found in [19,39,48].

Reducibilities are used to define complete sets and they
play a considerable role in understanding the relation of
sparse sets to circuit models, etc.

Definition. A set B is polynomial many-one reducible to a
set C (written $B \leq_m C$), if there is a function f computable in deterministic polynomial time satisfying $x \in B$ iff
$f(x) \in C$. A set B is polynomial Turing reducible to a set C
(written $B \leq_T C$), if there is a deterministic polynomial time

70

oracle Turing machine that accepts B when using oracle C.
We will generally use the terms many-one and Turing; and drop
the adjective polynomial.

Definition. A set C is many-one (Turing) complete for NP,
if C is in NP and every set in NP is many-one (Turing)
reducible to C. Similar properties define complete sets for
PTAPE, EXPTIME, etc.

   We begin with a few simple observations about how the number
of elements in a set grows with the size of the elements.

Definition. If A is a subset of Σ^*, we define the census
of A to be the function

$$C_A(n) = |A \cap \Sigma^{*n}|,$$

i.e., the exact number of elements of A of length up to n.

   Most of the sets with which we are familiar have an exponen-
tially growing census. For example, $C_{SAT}(n) \geq 2^{n^k}$ for some
k > 0. Furthermore, the census of SAT^c is also exponential.
Similar observations hold for all the known NP-complete,
PTAPE-complete, etc., sets.

Definition. A set A is dense if $C_A(n) \geq 2^{n^k}$ for some
k > 0.

   This property of denseness appears to naturally accompany
completeness of sets by virtue of their possessing padding

71

functions (as discussed in the next section). However, there is no proof that all complete sets have padding. This has led to various conjectures about the possibility that NP- (and other) complete sets might have a much smaller census, in particular, that such sets might be "sparse."

Definition. A set S is sparse if there is a polynomial p such that the number of strings in S up to length n, is at most p(n); i.e.,

$$C_S(n) \leq p(n).$$

We have already mentioned tally sets, which are subsets of 1* [6]. Obviously tally sets and their complements in 1* are both sparse.

In the next two sections we will examine first the circumstantial evidence for complete sets being dense. Then we shall show how sparse sets and various polynomial time reducibilities suggest different types of efficient algorithms for solving problems in classes such as NP or PTAPE.

Note. The polynomial many-one and Turing reductions are also called Karp and Cook reductions, after the authors who adapted the recursive many-one and Turing reductions to polynomial complexity [8,24].

3. P-ISOMORPHISMS, DENSE SETS, AND CONJECTURES ABOUT SPARSE SETS

The collection of known NP-complete sets taxes anyone's imagination. From SAT [8], to Traveling Salesman, CLIQUE, HAM and others [24], to the collection of over three hundred sets in [12] (and still growing [21]), we see a remarkable variety of NP-complete problems from logic, graph theory, automata theory, optimization, network design and other areas. Furthermore, many of these problems have been studied for approximations to their exact solutions; e.g., how close to an optimal traveling-salesman tour do various heuristics achieve. Here too, the methods and results vary widely with the problem area and point to the richness of the field.

In light of all this apparent variety, it is perhaps surprising that all these NP-complete problems are identical in a strong mathematical sense.

Definition [5]. We say that sets A and B are p-isomorphic if there is a reduction $f : A \leq_m B$ that is one-to-one, onto, and f^{-1}, the inverse, is polynomial time computable.

L. Berman and Hartmanis developed an easily applied method to show that a given NP-complete set is p-isomorphic to SAT by a method of padding functions.

Definition [5]. A set A has padding if there are two polynomial time computable functions p and d satisfying for all x, y,

(i) (padding) $p(x,y) \in A$ iff $x \in A$;

and

(ii) (decoding) $d(p(x,y)) = y$.

<u>Theorem</u> [5]. An NP-complete set A is p-isomorphic to SAT
if and only if A has padding.

This theorem has been applied to many known NP-complete
sets. For example, if the graph G is an instance of HAM
(the accepted inputs G are graphs to be checked for the
existence of a Hamiltonian circuit) and y is an arbitrary
string, then to compute a padding $p(G,y)$ in a most straightforward way, one would attach to G a subgraph G_y which
preserves the Hamiltonian circuit property. To assure decoding
when padding has been iterated, it suffices to attach the subgraph to G in a way that permits uniquely detecting the
attached subgraph G_y. The subgraph G_y must encode the
sybmols of y in a way that permits recovering y. Lastly,
note that membership in HAM is preserved. Several detailed
examples of this technique can be found in [5].

While this method of proving p-isomorphism is easy to use,
there is no general result that NP-completeness implies the
existence of padding; indeed, such a result would imply that
$P \neq NP$.

<u>Proposition</u> [5]. If all NP-complete sets are p-isomorphic,
then $P \neq NP$.

74

Proof. If P = NP, then finite sets are NP-complete under many-one reductions. But finite sets cannot be in one-to-one correspondence with infinite sets. □

Based on the evidence of so many p-isomorphic sets, Berman and Hartmanis were led to the following conjecture.

Conjecture 1. All the NP-complete sets are p-isomorphic.

Of course, proving the conjecture is at least as hard as proving P ≠ NP. In a weaker form, they gave the following.

Conjecture 2 (P-Isomorphism Conjecture). If P ≠ NP, then all the NP-complete sets are p-isomorphic.

From this second conjecture, one naturally considers how one might prove a set is not p-isomorphic to SAT; obviously, one method is to consider properties preserved under p-isomorphisms and then try to find sets which differ from SAT with respect to such a property. One such property examined in [5] is sparseness of sets. We observe, though, that sets with padding are dense since for $a \in A$, $p(a, \Sigma^n)$ generates 2^n strings in A of size polynomial in n, since p is invertible in the second argument. Further, p-isomorphism preserves sparseness. Thus sparse complete sets are natural candidates to refute the p-isomorphism conjectures without settling the P = NP question.

In a weaker form of the above Conjecture 2, they posed the following.

75

<u>Conjecture 3</u> (Sparse Set Conjecture). If P ≠ NP, then no NP-complete set can be sparse.

The bases of this conjecture are first, the belief that all NP-complete sets are p-isomorphic; second, the computational advantages that would ensue from sparse complete sets are unlikely (see next section); and third, that EXPTIME- and EXPTAPE-complete sets are provably not sparse (see Section 5).

<u>Notes</u>. 1. All the theorems and conjectures of this section apply as well to PTAPE-complete sets [5]. Reductions based on log-tape resource bounds, rather than polynomial time, are also studied; Hartmanis treats the isomorphisms of such in [14].

2. The p-isomorphism conjecture remains unsolved, but a number of additional results are known. Dowd [9] gives a general treatment of polynomial <u>cylinders</u> to develop basic material on p-isomorphisms. A very intriguing result there establishes that if a set is r.e. complete under polynomial, many-one reductions $(\leq_m)$, then it is complete under polynomial, one-one reductions. Thus only invertibility of these one-one reductions remains to be established in order to show that the p-isomorphism conjecture holds in the r.e. complete degree. Mahaney [34] showed that if the p-isomorphism conjecture does not hold, it fails badly: a polynomial, many-one degree (i.e., collection of $\leq_m$ equivalent sets) consists of either one p-isomorphism type (cohesive) or a countably infinite collection (split). Mahaney and Young [37] present this and related results on the orderings (under one-one, size increasing reductions) in degrees that split.

76

3. There are a number of interesting conjectures related to p-isomorphisms that seem tractable (i.e., they will not settle the P =? NP, or some similar difficult question) but are unsolved. The degree of P, and certain others obtained by diagonalization constructions, are known to split [37]. Can one construct a cohesive degree? Can one establish that some "natural" degree, e.g., EXPTIME-, NEXPTIME-, or EXPTAPE-complete sets, is cohesive or splits?

4. ARE SPARSE SETS HARD OR EASY IN COMPLEXITY?
We have established above that sparse sets give a significant structural deviation from the known NP-complete sets. Here we will outline two views on sparse sets: first, that sparse sets themselves might possess great intractability; second, that if NP-complete sets are reducible to sparse sets, then that reduction gives a computational advantage for solving NP in non-standard models of computing.

4.1 Translations
We have mentioned the P vs. NP vs. PTAPE questions repeatedly. At the more generous exponential resource levels, the corresponding questions are similarly intractable. We know that EXPTIME $\subseteq$ NEXPTIME $\subseteq$ EXTAPE but equalities or inequalities among these classes are not known. The following results show that separating these exponential classes implies separating P and NP by tally or sparse sets.

The first result is by Book [6] using translation arguments. Suppose that T is a set in 1*. Define a set E_T by the correspondence of $n \in E_T$ iff $1^n \in T$. (One can, as easily think of this as defining T from E_T.) The following result translates exponential time recognition to polynomial time recognition.

Theorem [6]. T is a tally set in NP - P (PTAPE - P) iff E_T is in NEXPTIME - EXPTIME (EXPTAPE - EXPTIME).

Thus, even tally sets might encode very intractable problems (assuming EXPTIME $\neq$ NEXPTIME).

These results are extended by Hartmanis, Immerman and Sewelson using a more refined translation coding [17]. From a sparse set S in NP, they code individual bits of each string in S as 5-tuples (n,k,i,j,b) in the exponential time set E_S; the five-tuple asserts that for strings of size n in S, there are k strings and in the ith string the jth bit is b. This correspondence gives the next theorem.

Theorem [17]. S is a sparse set in NP - P iff E_S is in NEXPTIME - EXPTIME.

Note. The translation of non-tally sets permits a refinement that distinguishes NP and co-NP in the presence of oracles. Two more translation results from [17] develop this.

Theorem. There is a sparse set in co-NP - P iff there is a set in Σ_2^E - EXPTIME.

Theorem [17]

    1. There is an oracle A for which NP(A) - P(A) has no sparse sets and co-NP(A) - P(A) has sparse sets.

    2. There is no oracle B for which co-NP(B) - P(B) has sparse sets and NP(B) - P(B) does not have sparse sets.

Of course, previous relativization results [2] have given oracles A which separate NP(A) and co-NP(A). This result gives a structural property for which NP and co-NP must differ.

While we are on the subject of relativizations, we must mention that Kurtz has used oracles to obtain the usual uncertainties about the existence of sparse sets in NP - P.

Theorem [26]. There is an oracle A such that there are sparse sets in NP(A) - P(A). There is an oracle B such that there are no sparse sets in NP(B) - P(B).

The oracle A can be the oracle separating P(A) from NP(A). The construction of B is a great deal more delicate as it requires separating P(B) and NP(B) while encoding all sparse sets to be accessible to deterministic computations.

4.2 Computational Advantages of Sparse Sets

From the above we have that, if $P \neq NP$, then sparse sets in NP - P correspond to intractable problems in NEXPTIME - EXPTIME. Thus, it is reasonable to expect them to be quite intractable. Nevertheless, we will show here that reducibility to sparse sets corresponds to significant computational

79

tractability.

Let us consider, for a moment, the question of why NP-complete sets are difficult to compute (assuming $P \neq NP$). We have mentioned already that Boolean formulas may be padded to generate other instances (preserving satisfiability). Is it possible that an NP-complete set consists of a few hard instances (i.e., sparse set) plus a dense collection of instances obtained by padding? If this were so, then we might have a sparse NP-complete set, if a reduction could decode to find the hard part and then query the sparse set. On the other hand, NP-complete sets might be hard because they contain many hard instances ([33,36] treat this in a general way).

Sparse many-one complete sets suggest a table-lookup model of feasible computing [5]. Suppose there is a sparse complete set S and a reduction f of SAT to S. To solve instances of SAT $\cap \Sigma^{*^n}$ we could have algorithms based on precomputation of a small amount of information and efficient interrogration of the precomputed data.

Assume that the reduction f with inputs from Σ^{*^n} reduces them to strings of size at most $q(n)$ and uses time $q'(n)$ where q and q' are polynomials. Further assume that the polynomial $p(n)$ bounds the census of S. First we precompute the elements of S up to size $q(n)$. The storage for such a table is polynomial in n: there are at most $p(q(n))$ strings of size at most $q(n)$ in the table.

Then, to solve instances $F \in SAT$ up to the given size, we could simply lookup $f(F) \in S$. After the precomputation, the

80

algorithm uses polynomial time: the computation of $f(F)$ is uniformly bounded by $q'(|F|)$ and searching the table is bounded by a small polynomial in $p(q(n))$ (depending on the organization of the table).

Of course, this is not a conventional notion of efficient algorithm--a finite program to solve all instances of SAT in Σ^*. Since the table depends on n, the algorithm has an infinite description; but, we only use a polynomial amount of it to solve problems. It is interesting that tables of polynomial bounded size (rather than 2^{n+1} bits for inputs of size up to n) could contain information to permit fast lookups to solve SAT.

The table-lookup above could be implemented as polynomial size circuits. We treat these circuits more generally.

Definition. A set has polynomial size circuits (abbreviated PSC here) if for some polynomial p there are circuits C_n of size (number of gates) at most $p(n)$ such that C_n computes the characteristic function of $A \cap \Sigma^n$.

An exact statement of the connection of sparse sets to circuits is due to Meyer [5].

Theorem. A set A has PSC iff A is polynomial time Turing reducible to a sparse set.

Two interesting classes of sets with PSC are R, random polynomial time, and BPP, bounded probabilistic polynomial time [1,13]. R is a subset of NP; BPP has recently been shown to be in the polynomial hierarchy [46]. An indication of the importance of R is that testing integers for compositeness is in R [42,47]. Both classes are defined by a property of "many witnesses" for members. Circuits are constructed by picking a small sequence of elements that witness many members.

The results above deal with the question of whether sets in the polynomial time hierarchy (other than those in P) might have polynomial size circuits. An even stronger requirement on these polynomial hierarchy classes is that all the sets have circuits $\{C_n\}$ with size uniformly bounded by a $O(n^k)$ for some k. A result by Kannan gives negative results for uniform size circuits.

Theorem [23]. For any k there is a set in $\Sigma_2^P \cap \Pi_2^P$ that does not have $O(n^k)$-size circuits.

Whether such sets might be in P or NP is unresolved. We conjecture that there might be sets in the polynomial hierarchy or PTAPE without polynomial size circuits at all.

Sparse sets appear in two more guises: almost polynomial time algorithms [38] which halt in polynomial time on all but a sparse set); and approximate algorithms [53] which may "lie" on a subset of inputs.

A special case of sparse sets occurs in tally languages; subsets of Σ^* when Σ has one letter [6]. They have the additional structure of being cosparse.

Underlying all these formalizations is a common theme: can a hard set be captured by a small amount of information? The

82

results in the next two sections all address this question.

Note. There are a great many closely related notions of circuit and sparseness that lie outside our subject: circuit complexity is a far more extensive field than we indicate; sets with "gaps" of no elements are sometimes called sparse [28,29].

5. MANY-ONE REDUCIBILITIES TO SPARSE SETS

In this section we examine polynomial many-one reductions to sparse sets. This is the strongest reducibility and gives the strongest results.

The first results by Meyer (reported in [5]) were based on diagonalization.

Theorem. There are no sparse complete sets for EXPTIME, NEXPTIME, or EXPTAPE.

Remark. The diagonalization constructs a set A such that for every polynomial reduction f_i, either f_i is 1-1 almost everywhere, or if $f_i(x) = f_i(y)$ occurs sufficiently often, then it diagonalizes with $x \in A$ and $y \notin A$. To further assure that A is dense and co-dense poses no problem. A similar proof based on $n/\log(n)$ tape simulation of linear time reductions gave the following.

Theorem [5]. A sparse set cannot be a hardest CSL under linear time reductions.

The remainder of the results in this section develop efficient algorithms based on sparse sets. For convenience we choose SAT as the canonical NP-complete set.

The idea of a self-reducibility for satisfiability of Boolean formulas is that the membership problem $F \in SAT$ is reduced to SAT membership problems for smaller sized Boolean formulas. We use the following self-reduction of SAT:

For a Boolean formula $F = F(x_1, \ldots, x_n)$ we define F_0 and F_1 to be F with false and true substituted for x_1 respectively. Also perform trivial simplifications (e.g., x_2 and false simplifies to false, etc.).

This self-reducibility is called disjunctive, i.e., that F is satisfiable if and only if F_0 or F_1 is satisfiable. The self-reduction gives rise to a search tree by considering iterations of the above operation: F_x for $x \in \{0,1\}^*$; observe that F is satisfiable if and only if some leaf simplifies to true.

The first result, presented at ICALP in 1978 by P. Berman, introduced a powerful tree search technique that has been most useful. We first describe results based on this technique and then give a proof in detail.

Theorem [4]. Let f be a polynomial-time many-one reduction of SAT to S^c (i.e., so that $f(SAT^c) \subset S$) satisfying

$$|f(\Sigma^{*n})| \leq p(n)$$

for some polynomial $p(\ )$. Then SAT is in P.

Berman originally stated these results for CLIQUE and in a general form relating the density of $f(\Sigma^{*n})$ to the recognition time. The sparse set prunes the search tree away from unsatisfiable formulas by the observation that if $s \in S$ is known and $f(F_x) = s$, then, since F_x is unsatisfiable, there is no need to search below F_x. Fortune showed that the tree search essentially used only the reducibility of SAT^c to a sparse set, but it had no requirements on the reduced values of SAT. He also extended the methods to PTAPE-complete sets.

Theorem [11]. If there is a sparse co-NP-complete set S, then P = NP.

Theorem [11]. If f is a reduction of a PTAPE-complete set (e.g., QBF) such that

$$|f(\Sigma^{*n})| \leq p(n)$$

for some polynomial p, then P = PTAPE.

These tree search methods are refined further in [38] by generalizing self-reducibility: a language L is self-reducible if a polynomial time oracle TM decides $x \in L$ using elements of L "smaller" than x as the oracle. The notion of smaller in [38] is a well founded ordering on strings such that the longest chain below x has at most polynomial in $|x|$ elements. The most common example is induced by the length of strings. Further, by clarifying conjunctive self-reducibility (as illustrated by SAT^c: F is unsatisfiable iff

F_0 and F_1 are unsatisfiable) more general statements were possible.

Theorem [38]

1. If L is self-reducible and L and L^c are many-one reducible to sparse sets, then L is in P.

2. If L is conjunctively self-reducible and many-one reducible to a sparse set, then L is in P.

The latter result applies to many sets in co-NP not known to be complete, such as a modified form of integer primality testing or the complement of GRAPH-ISOMORPHISM. This raises the possibility that sparse reducibilities might be used to prove membership in P, even though P ≠ NP. For example, any sparse set with conjunctive self-reducibility is in P.

Let us turn to P. Berman's algorithm that proves these results. We will prove the refined statement due to Fortune: If SAT^c is many-one reducible to a sparse set S, then P = NP. There are three ideas behind the algorithm. The first is a depth-first search of the tree of self-reductions of a formula F whose satisfiability is to be decided. The search will either find a leaf <u>true</u> (establishing that the path to that leaf indicates a satisfying assignment) or it will establish that all leaves are <u>false</u> (and the formula F is unsatisfiable).

Since the tree is quite large ($2^{n+1} - 1$ nodes if F has n variables) we will use a subset of S, the sparse set, as a "stop list" for the search. If a node F_x is encountered in

86

the tree search and $f(F_x)$ is on the stop list, then F_x is
unsatisfiable, so the search does not go below that node. Since
S is sparse, the stop list will be sufficiently small, and the
use of it will reduce the number of unsatisfiable nodes visited
while permitting the search to fall through to a satisfying
assignment if such an assignment exists.

Now, observe that S is co-NP-complete, and thus a stop
list will not be straightforward to construct. The list is
built up during the search by a rule based on the conjunctive
self-reducibility of SAT^c. To begin, we put $f(\underline{false})$ on the
stop list. Suppose a formula G such that $f(G)$ is not on
the stop list is encountered in the search. If G_0 and G_1
are found to be unsatisfiable, then G is also unsatisfiable,
so $f(G)$ can be put on the stop list. Thus, the stop list
begins with $f(\underline{false})$ and grows by applications of this conjunctive self-reducibility rule.

Proof of the Theorem. The following algorithm, decide(F),
will determine the satisfiability of a Boolean formula F in
polynomial time. The procedure search(G) will halt if a
satisfying assignment is found; if it returns, then G is
unsatisfiable.

87

```
decide(F):
    SL := {f(false)};
    search(F);
    /* reaching here implies F is unsatisfiable */
    print "Unsatisfiable";
    end decide;

search(G):
    if G = true
        then do
            print "Satisfiable";
            halt;
            end;
    if f(G) is in SL
        then
            return;    /* G is unsatisfiable */
        else do        /* search below G */
            search(G_0);
            search(G_1);
            /* reaching here implies G_0 and G_1 are
                unsatisfiable */
            /* so G is unsatisfiable also */
            add f(G) to SL;
            return;
            end;
        end search;
```

Obviously, if $\underline{search}$(G) finds a satisfying assignment, it reports such, and is correct. To see that $\underline{search}$ is correct when it reports "unsatisfiable," observe that it searches every formula, except under those G reducing $f(G) \in SL$. If $SL \subset S$, we are guaranteed such formulas G are unsatisfiable. But, SL is initialized to {f(false)}; and every value added to SL is in S by observations above. This establishes correctness of search and decide.

We now establish the running time of this search algorithm. Assume F has m variables. Let p bound the density of S and let q be a monotonic polynomial bounding the increases in length under the reduction f. Then the algorithm above visits at most

$$m + (m * p(q(|F|)))$$

interior nodes of the tree. The total number of nodes visited is at most twice that.

To see this, suppose G and G' are two unsatisfiable formulas in the tree with the same reduced value (i.e., $f(G) = f(G')$) occurring in the interior (i.e., not as leaves) of the pruned search tree. Then they must be on the same branch from the root. Otherwise, one formula, say G, would be searched first; its reduced value $f(G)$ would be determined to be in S; and the depth-first search would not go below G', contradicting the assumption that G' is not a leaf.

Thus the number of distinct paths from the root to unsatisfiable interior nodes is bounded by the number of values in S that $f(G)$ can take, which is at most $p(q(|F|))$. Since the

tree has height m, there are at most $m*p(q(|F|))$ interior
unsatisfiable nodes with reduced values in S. A satisfying
assignment might visit at most another m interior nodes in the
search.

We now have that a polynomial number of nodes are visited
and examination of the algorithm shows a polynomial time computation at each node. Thus the algorithm recognizes SAT in
polynomial time. This completes the proof of the theorem. □

The results of Fortune, Meyer and Paterson, mentioned above,
are all refinements on this search method of P. Berman's. These
results seem to reach the limit of applying the tree search
method originating in [4].

The reason that they do not apply to <u>disjunctively</u> self-
reducible problems (e.g., SAT: F is satisfiable iff F_0 <u>or</u>
F_1 is satisfiable) is that there is no guaranteed pruning of
the search tree. The disjunctive (NP) problem seeks a single
witness path in the search tree. The sparse set corresponding
to the co-NP-problem prunes away useless unsatisfiable subtrees
by the coincidence of reduced values in the sparse set. A
sparse set for SAT would lack any direct method to avoid
large unsatisfiable subtrees.

These results leave open the original conjecture by
Hartmanis and L. Berman, that there are no sparse NP-complete
sets unless P = NP. Hartmanis and Mahaney attempted to over-
come this by additional requirements on the sparse set. While
these results seem to "throw hypotheses at the problem until it
succumbs," they also provide an instructive outline to the

90

methods that do solve the problem. The following definition and three theorems are from [15,16].

Definition. We say that a set S has easy census if the census $C_S(n)$ is computable in time polynomial in n.

Theorem. Suppose S is a sparse set in NP with easy census. Then S^c is in NP.

Proof. The following enumeration algorithm recognizes x in S^c in nondeterministic polynomial time.

```
sc(x):
    n := |x|;
    k := C_S(n);
    Guess s_1, s_2, ..., s_k that are of size < n,
        and all distinct;
    For all i check that s_i ∈ S with a nondeterministic
        polynomial time computation;
    Accept x if x is not among the s_i's;
end sc;
```

Clearly for an input x of size n, the algorithm enumerates all elements of S up to size n and checks that the input x is not among them; thus correctness is obvious. The complexity is bounded by guessing polynomially many s_i's and their witnesses, and checking a polynomial time predicate of x, the s_i's and their witnesses. Thus, S^c is in NP. □

Theorem. Suppose S is a sparse NP-complete set with easy census. Then NP = co-NP.

Proof. Any set in co-NP is reducible to S^c which is in NP by the above theorem. □

Theorem. If S is a sparse NP-complete set with easy census, then P = NP.

Proof. Reducing SAT to S is equivalent to reducing SAT^c to S^c. Since S^c is in NP it can be reduced to S which is NP-complete. Composing reductions SAT^c to S^c to S establishes the hypothesis of Fortune's version of Berman's Theorem; we conclude P = NP. □

Hartmanis and Mahaney observed, however, that no interesting sets with easily computable census are known. It is not always the case that unrealistic hypotheses are useless, though.

In his PH.D. thesis, Mahaney solved the original conjecture [32,35]. The principal new observation is that since the census of a sparse set is bounded by a polynomial, constructions implicit in the above three theorems can be tried for every possible value of the census.

There are three steps to the development above:

1. given the easy census, prove NP = co-NP;

2. compose reductions of SAT^c to S^c to S, given 1; and

3. with the reduction of 2, perform the tree search algorithm.

92

Direct analogies to this are not possible when trying various census values. The enumeration method of the theorems above, used with a guess that $C_S(n) = k$, at best gives locally (i.e., for inputs of some particular size n) "NP = co-NP" if we have the right k. (We use the quote marks to indicate dubiousness.)

The critical matter is in step 2: S^c is shown to be in NP and thus reducible to S. Without the census, we cannot obtain that S^c is in NP, and thus, cannot uniformly construct reductions for step 3. We will replace S^c in this role with a new set in NP, the pseudocomplement of S, which incorporates all the feasible guesses of the census of S into inputs. The pseudocomplement permits constructing many reductions for step 3 and allows a uniform polynomial time bound for multiple searches.

This discussion leads to the following result.

Theorem [32,35]. If there is a sparse NP-complete set, then P = NP.

Proof. We begin with the pseudocomplement of S, denoted PC(S). The inputs to pc, the acceptor of PC(S) are s, a string which is a candidate to belong to S^c; k, a guess of the census $C_S(n)$; and 0^n, a dual purpose argument that both indicates n and pads the input to ensure that the procedure operates in nondeterministic polynomial time.

We define pc by the following procedure:

```
pc(x,k,0ⁿ):
begin
    Reject if |x| > n or k > p(n);
    Guess s₁, ..., sₖ of length at most n such that
        all are distinct;
    For all i check that sᵢ ∈ S with a nondeterministic
        polynomial time computation;
    Accept x if x is not among the sᵢ's;
end;
```

Let $|x| \leq n$ and $k \leq p(n)$. Then on input $(x,k,0^n)$ the nondeterministic machine pc will

(a)   accept if $k < C_S(n)$;

(b)   reject if $k > C_S(n)$; and

(c)   if $k = C_S(n)$, then pc accepts if and only if $x \in S^c$.

Intuitively, for the correct guess, $k = C_S(n)$, pc is a recognizer of S^c. Moreover, pc accepts its language in non-deterministic polynomial time. Note that the input 0^n in a padded form is used to ensure this since $|x| + |k|$ may be less than n, but the algorithm guesses and verifies up to $p(n)$ elements of S of size up to n.

Next we construct the functions required to prune the tree searches. In Berman's search, only one function is used and it is a reduction of SAT^c to S. Here we will use a family of function fragments for many searches. One of these "pruning functions" will in fact be a reduction of finite fragments of

SAT^C to the sparse set S, but knowing which one it is requires knowing the elusive census.

The following discussion shows how such functions are constructed from the sparse NP-complete set S and many-one reductions of PC(S) to S and of SAT to S.

Since PC(S) is in NP and S is NP-complete, there is a polynomial-time many-one reduction of the pseudo-complement to S

$$g \; : \; PC(S) \longrightarrow S$$

and a monotonic polynomial q, so that inputs to pc of length n are reduced to strings of length at most q(n) [8,24]. Similarly, for the NP-complete problem SAT, there is a polynomial-time many-one reduction

$$h \; : \; SAT \longrightarrow S$$

and a monotonic polynomial r bounding the increase in length.

Let F of length m be a Boolean formula whose satisfiability is to be decided and let n = r(m). Then for any formula F' occurring in the tree of all self-reductions of F we have

$$|h(F')| \; \le \; r(|F'|) \; \le \; r(|F|) \; = \; r(m) \; = \; n$$

since $|F'| \le |F|$.

Recall that we want the pruning function to map SAT^c to the sparse set S. Certainly, $h(SAT^c) \subseteq S^c$. Then if $k = C_S(n)$ we have that

$$g(h(SAT^c \cap \Sigma*^m), k, 0^n) \subseteq S$$

since g reduces the pseudo-complement of S to S. The following diagram summarizes this:

$$SAT^c \cap \Sigma*^m \rightarrow (S^c, C_S(n), 0^n) \rightarrow S.$$

Of course, if $k \neq C_S(n)$, then the inclusion into S does not hold; we are simply mapping strings into $\Sigma*$.

Since we do not know the true census, we incorporate guesses of it into a set of pruning functions. We define for each n and each $k \leq p(n)$

$$f_{n,k}(F') = f(F', n, k) = g(h(F'), k, 0^n)$$

which will be a pruning function.

Claim. Let F be of size m, F' of size $\leq m$, and n and k bounded as indicated above; then

   (a) f is polynomial time computable, and thus:
   (b) $f_{n,k}(F')$ uses computation time bounded by a polynomial
        in m;

96

(c) for $k = C_S(n)$, F' is unsatisfiable if and only if
$f_{n,k}(F')$ is in S; and

(d) for $k = C_S(n)$, the unsatisfiable formulas of length
at most m are mapped by $f_{n,k}$ to at most

$$p(q(2n + c'\log(n))) \leq p(q(3n))$$

distinct strings of S where c' is a constant depending only on p.

Proof. Parts (a) and (b) are immediate since the pruning
function is composed from polynomial-time reductions. Part (c)
follows from the discussion above. For part (d) observe that

$$2n + c'\log(n) \leq 3n$$

is a bound on the length of $(h(F'), k, 0^n)$. Applying pq
gives an upper bound on the census of strings in S that the
triple could map onto. □

The last step of proving the Theorem modifies the tree search
method. If we knew $C_S(n)$ we could simply perform the search
with $f_{n,C_S(n)}$. However, we only know that a suitable value for
k exists. The modified search algorithm tries $f_{n,k}$ for all
$k \leq p(n)$. For certain values of k, the tree search may
attempt to visit too many nodes. Part (d) of the Claim and the
analysis of the number of nodes searched by Berman's tree search
give a polynomial bound on the number of nodes that might be

visited: if the search exceeds $m + m*p(q(3r(m)))$ interior nodes visited, then we can conclude $k \neq C_S(n)$.

Let F be a Boolean formula of length m and $n = r(m)$. Then the following algorithm decides the satisfiability of F and runs in deterministic polynomial time.


```
        decide(F):
            For k = 0 to p(r(m)) do
                Execute the depth-first search using pruning
                    function f_{n,k}(F') at each node F' encountered
                    in the pruned search tree;
                If a leaf with formula true is found
                then halt; {F is satisfiable}
                If a tree search visits more than m + m*p(q(3r(m)))
                    interior nodes,
                then
                    halt the search for this k;
                end;
            /* F is not satisfiable */
            end decide;
```


The algorithm clearly runs in polynomial time since the loop is executed at most $p(r(m))$ times and each iteration of the loop visits at most a polynomial (in m) number of nodes. At each node visited, evaluating $f_{n,k}$ requires polynomial time.

The following claim establishes the correctness of the algorithm.

98

Claim. If F is satisfiable, then for $k = C_S(r(m))$ the
search will find a satisfying assignment. If F is unsatisfiable, then no value of k will yield a satisfying assignment.

Proof. By the previous Claim, $k = C_S(r(m))$ gives a pruning
function that maps the unsatisfiable formulas of length at most
m to a polynomially bounded set. We argued above that Berman's
depth-first search will find a satisfying assignment visiting at
most

$$m + (m * p(q(3r(m))))$$

internal nodes. The second statement is obvious. □

The correctness of this polynomial-time decision procedure
for SAT given a sparse NP-complete set completes the proof
of the Theorem. □

The original conjecture of Berman-Hartmanis is that no NP-
complete set can be sparse. The results of this section essentially confirm the conjecture (unless P = NP). They also show
that sparse many-one complete sets can provide no computational
advantage for NP or co-NP-complete sets.

What about sets in NP or co-NP that may not be complete?
Ladner establishes that such sets exist if $P \neq NP$ [28]. We
have already discussed translations of sets in NEXPTIME -
EXPTIME as candidates [6,17], and the relativization results
[26,17].

What about sets with a self-reducibility property? Recall the result of Meyer and Paterson that if the complement of GRAPH-ISOMORPHISM is reducible to a sparse set then GRAPH-ISOMORPHISM is in P. What if GRAPH-ISOMORPHISM is reducible to a sparse set S?

The construction of the pseudo-complement can proceed as above; however, the remainder of the proof used the NP-completeness of S to construct a reduction of PC(S) to S. Since GRAPH-ISOMORPHISM is not known to be NP-complete, and thus S is not assumed to be NP-complete, the proof fails at that point in the construction. It would be interesting to remedy this. Apparently, this would require some sort of reducibility to GRAPH-ISOMORPHISM, but not necessarily NP-completeness.

6. TURING REDUCIBILITIES, SPARSE SETS, AND CIRCUITS

In this section we examine Turing reducibilities to sparse sets. Since Turing reducibilities are apparently stronger than many-one ($A \leq_m B$ implies $A \leq_T B$, but the converse is not known), we expect weaker conclusions than those in Section 5, and even the possibility that NP-complete sets are Turing reducible to sparse sets, but not many-one reducible to sparse sets. Both expectations are borne out; of course, the distinctions are established by relativizations. Finally, we examine restricted Turing reductions to sparse sets.

6.1 Turing Reductions

We have already mentioned that polynomial-time Turing (Cook) reducibility to a sparse set is equivalent to having polynomial size circuits (abbreviated PSC). These are special cases of a more general notion developed by Karp and Lipton in [25]. This generalizes the idea that polynomial size circuits provide $p(n)$ bits of "advice" for inputs of size n ($p(\ )$ is some polynomial) and evaluation of the circuit is a polynomial time computation.

They consider classes K/S, where K is a class of computations (P, PTAPE, etc.), and S is a class of size functions bounding the amount of advice. An advice function for S, $a(n)$ must satisfy that there is some $s \in S$ such that

$$|a(n)| \leq s(n).$$

(Note that we do not restrict the computation time of $a(\ )$.) Then by K/S ("sets accepted in K with advice S") we denote the class containing sets

$$\{x : R(x, a(|x|))\ \text{is true}\}$$

where R is some predicate in K and $a(\ )$ is an advice function for S. We will mainly consider S the bound on advice to be polynomial or logarithmic (denoted poly and log), and K to be classes such as P or PTAPE.

The first result we mention puts P/poly in the context of
our previous discussions. Equivalence of 1 and 2 is in [5],
and 1 and 3 is in [40].

Theorem. The following are equivalent:
   1. C has polynomial size circuits.
   2. C is Turing reducible to a sparse set.
   3. C is in P/poly.

It is well known that sets with bounded uniform complexity
(e.g., in P) have PSC, which is a non-uniform notion of
efficient computation. Karp and Lipton derive results from
structural properties of sets that give converses: if complete
sets have non-uniform tractability, then those sets (or related
sets) will have uniform bounds on their complexity.

We noted in Section 5 that SAT has self-reducibility.
Complete sets in NP or PTAPE, etc., can be defined by self-
reducibilities or recurrences on smaller members. Then polynomial size circuits for such sets can be guessed and verified
by a "bootstrap" or "recursive definition" technique. Let us
examine such a result for NP in detail.

Suppose that SAT is accepted by a collection $\{C_n\}$ of
polynomial size circuits which, we can assume, are encoded in
some standard way as strings and that C_n will recognize all
strings in SAT up to size n; i.e., if F of size $\leq$ n is
satisfiable, then $C_n(F) = 1$ and if F is unsatisfiable, then
$C_n(F) = 0$. In general it may be hard to find such circuits or
distinguish circuits that are correct for SAT from those that

are not. Consider the recognition problem for the set of good circuits

      GC = {(C,n) : C is a correct circuit for SAT for
           all formulas F : |F| $\leq$ n}.

It is immediate that GC is in Π_2^P but defining SAT through self-reducibility and the circuit gives a Π_1^P characterization:

      (C,n) is in GC if and only if
          C(true) = 1
        and C(false) = 0
        and $\forall$ F of size up to n
          C(F) = 1 iff (C(F_0) = 1 or C(F_1) = 1).

We can then use a guess and verify strategy to find good circuits by fitting

      $\exists$(C,n) . . . $\forall$ F . . . (c,n) $\in$ GC

into sentences that characterize sets in the polynomial time hierarchy. For example, consider a set L in Σ_3^P characterized by

      w $\in$ L iff $\exists$ x $\forall$y $\exists$ z P(w,x,y,z) where P is some polynomial time predicate. We will suppress stating the polynomially bounded character of the quantifiers in such sentences. By Cook's theorem, reducing problems in NP to satisfiability of Boolean formulas, we know there is a polynomial time function BF_P depending on the predicate P, satisfying for all w, x and y:

$$\exists \; z \; P(w,x,y,z) \quad iff \quad BF_P(w,x,y) \quad is \; satisfiable.$$

We see then, that:

$$w \in L \quad iff \; \exists \; x \; \forall \; y \; \exists \; z \; P(w,x,y,z)$$
$$iff \; \exists \; x \; \forall \; y \; BF_P(w,x,y) \quad is \; satisfiable$$
$$iff \; \exists \; (C,n), \; x \; \forall \; F, \; y \; ((C,n) \in GC \quad and$$
$$C(BF_P(w,x,y)) = 1).$$

This two quantifier characterization of L proves that $L \in \Sigma_2^P$. This illustrates a general technique for eliminating additional quantifier alternations when circuits exist. We have specifically proven a result due to Karp, Lipton and Sipser.

<u>Theorem</u> [25]. If NP has polynomial size circuits, then $\Sigma_2^P = \Pi_2^P$.

We have mentioned R, random polynomial time, which is a subset of NP. If a set A is in R, then membership can be tested with high confidence by guessing several witnesses. Were NP = R, that would give useful tractability to NP. But R

has polynomial size circuits [1], so NP = R implies $\Sigma_2^P = \Pi_2^P$.
Thus, NP = R has such strong consequences that it is considered unlikely.

A technique similar to the above proof can be applied to PTAPE. The set QBF of quantified Boolean formulas (formulas: $Q_1 x_1 \, Q_2 x_2 \, \ldots \, F(x_1, x_2, \ldots)$ where each Q_i is either $\forall$ or $\exists$ and the formula is in QBF if it is true) is a complete set for PTAPE. It is straightforward to develop a self-reducibility for QBF. Define F_0 and F_1 to be F with the leading quantifier $Q_1 x_1$ eliminated and x_1 substituted with false and true, respectively; the self-reducibility statement is similar to that for SAT, simply being careful that existential quantifiers require membership in either reduced formula and universal quantifiers require membership for both reduced formulas. We can then define a predicate of good circuits for QBF, and similarly prove the following theorem.

Theorem [25]. If PTAPE has polynomial size circuits, then PTAPE = $\Sigma_2^P = \Pi_2^P$.

A stronger results holds for EXPTIME.

Theorem (Meyer in [25]). If EXPTIME has polynomial size circuits, then EXPTIME = $\Sigma_2^P \neq P$.

These results establish that polynomial size circuits for NP or PTAPE are unlikely (given our bias that the polynomial hierarchy does not collapse at all) but the evidence is not as strong as that against sparse many-one complete sets. Viewed as observations about computational models, we have that the table-lookup model is equivalent to ordinary polynomial time for solving NP-complete problems. The results for the PSC model do not clarify the relative power to solve complete problems.

These methods have been extended by Yap [52], and Balcázar, Book, and Schöning [3]. [52] follows [25] in the style of proof; [3] follows the presentation here. Both papers obtain this theorem.

Theorem. If there is a sparse oracle S such that $\Sigma_k^P(S) = \Pi_k^P(S)$, then $\Sigma_{k+2}^P = \Pi_{k+2}^P$.

Balcázar, Book, and Schöning use this to obtain this result: The polynomial hierarchy PH does not collapse iff for every sparse set PH(S) does not collapse. Related results addressing the question of structure of oracles for relativizations results are in [31].

A second approach to these non-uniform classes, called the "round robin tournament" method is also in [25]. It is not clear whether it might be subsumed by the above method of recursive definition. We outline an example here, for completeness.

If a class of sets is defined by alternating games [7] as for P and PTAPE, then a non-uniform bound can be treated as the existence of a winning strategy encoded in some sparse oracle. Proofs take the form of guessing the advice that wins against all other advice. For example, Karp and Lipton give a two quantifier characterization of PTAPE.

We will develop this for the game of HEX, a complete set
for PTAPE [10]. Inputs are positions consisting of a graph
with two designated nodes, two sets of nodes belonging to two
players (S1 and S2), and the number of the player whose
turn it is. The players alternate picking an heretofore un-
chosen node for their respective sets. Player 1 wins if a path
using nodes from S1 exists between the designated nodes;
player 2 wins otherwise. The recognition problem is the set of
positions from which the first player can force a win.

HEX = {P : player 1 can win from position P}.

Now, suppose that HEX is polynomial Turing reducible to a
sparse oracle (i.e., is in P/poly). Given a position P of
size n, only oracle questions of some polynomial size in n
can be queried. The strings in the sparse oracle up to that
size can be encoded into a string W_n whose size is bounded by
a polynomial q(n). Player 1 can use that string to play a
winning strategy for HEX. Assume player 1 is in a position P
for which player 1 has a winning strategy; try each move until
a move is found such that any response by player 2 leads to a
position P' in which player 1 again has a winning strategy.
Player 1 makes that move. The computations to determine the
move are polynomial time computable. This strategy guarantees
a win if started in a position with a winning strategy. Thus,
there is a small description of a winning strategy; i.e., a
string W_n that can be used to derive a winning strategy for

any position P of size n from which player 1 can win. W_n
is a string with size polynomially bounded in n. Similarly,
if a position does not have a winning strategy, then no string
L_n as advice can give a win against a winning strategy. We can
now characterize

$$HEX = \{P : \exists\ W_n\ \forall\ L_n\ \text{player 1 using } W_n \text{ beats player 2}$$
$$\text{using } L_n\}$$

with the usual boundedness of quantifiers suppressed. This
sentence with two alternations, proves that HEX is in Σ_2^P.
This gives the same result as above.

Theorem [25]. If PTAPE is in P/poly, then $\Sigma_2^P = \Pi_2^P$ = PTAPE.

   Other results by this technique include the following.

Theorem [25]
   1. If PSPACE is in P/log, then PSPACE = P.
   2. If NP is in P/log, then P = NP.
   3. If EXPTIME is in PSPACE/poly, then EXPTIME = PSPACE.

   Generally, the consequences of Turing reducibility to sparse
sets are weaker than for many-one reducibility. Although
stronger results would be much appreciated for elegance and
completeness, relativization cautions as follows.

Theorem
   1. There is an oracle A such that NP has PSC, but
P ≠ NP [27,20].

108

2. There is an oracle A such that NP has PSC, but $\Sigma_2^P \neq \Sigma_1^P$ [20].

Strengthened versions of 2 were obtained by Heller [18] and Wilson [51].

6.2 Restricted Turing Reducibilities

Further work in this area follows divergent themes: stronger conditions on the sparse set, stronger reducibilities, and applications to other complexity classes.

One can easily see from the construction in [5] that if SAT has a sparse oracle, then it has a sparse oracle in Σ_2^P. The stronger assumption that the oracle be in NP gives the following.

Theorem [32]. If SAT is Turing reducible to a sparse set in NP, then $\Delta_2^P = \Sigma_2^P = \Pi_2^P$. Long gives an elegant treatment of this to show the next result.

Theorem [30]

1. If SAT is Turing reducible to a sparse set in Δ_2^P, then $\Delta_2^P = \Sigma_2^P = \Pi_2^P$.
2. If SAT is Turing reducible to a sparse or cosparse set in NP, then $\Delta_2^P = \Sigma_2^P = \Pi_2^P$.

When stronger conditions are placed on the reductions, sharper conclusions are possible. Papers by Yap, Yesha, and Ukkonen examine common restricted reducibilities. The proofs of these theorems extend the tree search methods of [4] and [32].

Theorem [49,52]. If A is complete for co-NP and A is conjunctively Turing reducible to a sparse set, then A is in P.

Theorem [53]. If A is complete for NP, co-NP, or PTAPE and A is bounded, positive, truth-table reducible to a sparse set, then A is in P.

Theorem [49]

1. If A is complete for NP or PTAPE and A is bounded Turing reducible to a tally set, then A is in P.

2. If A is complete for PTAPE and A is conjunctively Turing reducible to a sparse set, then A is in P.

One attempt to give a general extension of these methods is in [45,36]. First, they examine gamma and random reducibilities, which are not known to be restricted Turing reducibilities. (The result for SAT^C and gamma reducibility is also in [52].)

Theorem [36]. If SAT or SAT^C is gamma or random reducible to a sparse set, then NP = co-NP. If a gamma complete set has PSC, then $\Sigma_4^P = \Pi_4^P$.

Second, they introduce polynomial self-reducibility, which allows bounded alternations of quantification over smaller elements of the set. This is used to characterize classes in PTAPE that are defined by counting [13,44]. As an example applied to a problem that typifies counting [50],

110

EXACT = {(F,k) | Boolean formula F has exactly k
                  satisfying assignments}

has "Σ_1^P" self-reducibility by (F,k) $\in$ EXACT   if and only if

    F = true   and k = 1
or
    F = false   and k = 0
or
    there exist k_0 and k_1 such that

        $k_0 + k_1 = k$

        and (F_0,k_0) in EXACT
        and (F_1,k_1) in EXACT.

Their main result extends the methods based on self-
reducibility.

Theorem [45,36]
    1. If a set has polynomial self-reducibility and is re-
ducible (many-one, Turing, gamma, or random) to a sparse set,
then it is in the polynomial hierarchy.
    2. If a set has polynomial self-reducibility and is NP or
co-NP-hard, then the polynomial hierarchy collapses (to a level
depending on the type of reduction to a sparse set and the polynomial self-reducibility).

111

An interesting question arises about the applicability of this theorem. Almost all of the results in this survey begin with an "If pigs could fly" hypothesis. But consider BPP [13] which is known to have PSC (equivalently, Turing reducibility to a sparse set). If a self-reducibility could be found for BPP sets, then 1, above, would give yet another proof that BPP is in the polynomial hierarchy [46]. All the other sets examined have self-reducibility, but not sparse reducibility.

SUMMARY

We outlined two broad reasons for examination of sparse sets. The first is that they offered some hope of establishing tractability for classes such as NP (weaker than P = NP). The second is to explore the analogy with the work on immune sets that illuminated the structure of the r.e. sets. With these motives, this paper has examined recent work considering the existence of sparse sets in NP, PTAPE, etc., and the consequences of reducing complete sets to sparse sets.

The general conclusion on the tractability issue must be that reducibility to sparse sets is either useless or unlikely. For example, in the Berman and Mahaney results, it implies P = NP, anyway. For the Karp and Lipton results, the consequences of Turing reducibility to sparse sets are very strong collapses of the polynomial hierarchy.

As for illuminating the structure of sets in NP, PTAPE, etc., the work appears most successful. New questions and new techniques have greatly extended our knowledge about relativizations, p-isomorphisms, the P vs. NP question and its

112

relation to EXPTIME vs. NEXPTIME, the structure (e.g., self-reducibility) of complete sets, and many other questions.

We expect that examining these basic structural questions for computational complexity will continue to illuminate the broad development of many areas in computer science.

ACKNOWLEDGMENTS
I would particularly like to thank Ronald V. Book at the University of California at Santa Barbara for initiating and arranging the Conference on Computational Complexity Theory at which this material was presented as an invited talk. The chore of organizing the material became my valuable opportunity to reorganize it and to develop a better understanding of the results presented here. The theme of the conference brought together participants who were especially capable of adding insight to the study of computational complexity theory in their presentations and timely comments. Professor Book's tireless efforts made it all work.

Quite a few people have commented on presentation and drafts of this paper. The ones I remember include José Balcázar, Ronald Book, Juris Hartmanis, Neil Immerman, Stuart Kurtz, Jeff Lagarias, Timothy Long, Albert Meyer, Uwe Schöning, Alan Selman, Vivian Sewelson, Janos Simon, Michael Sipser, Celia Wrathall, Ann Yasuhara, Paul Young, and two anonymous referees. Any errors or omissions are mine.

This research was partially supported by the National Science Foundation under Grant No. MCS82-15544.

REFERENCES

[1] Adleman, L., Two theorems on random polynomial-time. Proceedings of the 19th IEEE Symposium on Foundations of Computer Science (1978), 75-83.

[2] Baker, T., Gill, J., and Solovay, R., Relativizations of the P = NP question. SIAM Journal on Computing 4(1975), 431-442.

[3] Balcázar, J., Book, R., and Schöning, U., The polynomial-time hierarchy and sparse oracles. Journal of the Association for Computing Machinery, to appear.

[4] Berman, P., Relationships between density and deterministic complexity of NP-complete languages. Proceedings of the 5th International Colloquium on Automata, Languages, and Programming, Lecture Notes in Computer Science 62(1978), 63-71.

[5] Berman, P. and Hartmanis, J., On isomorphisms and density of NP and other complete sets. SIAM Journal on Computing 6(1977), 305-322. Also in Proceedings of the 8th ACM Symposium on Theory of Computing (1976), 30-40.

[6] Book, R., Tally languages and complexity classes. Information and Control 26(1974), 186-193.

[7] Chandra, A., Kozen, D., and Stockmeyer, L., Alternation. Journal of the Association for Computing Machinery 28 (1981), 114-133.

[8] Cook, S., The complexity of theorem proving procedures. Proceedings of the 3rd ACM Symposium on Theory of Computing (1971), 151-158.

[9] Dowd, M., On isomorphism. Technical Report, Rutgers University (1978).

[10] Even, S. and Tarjan, R.E., A combinatorial problem which is complete in polynomial space. Proceedings of the 7th ACM Symposium on Theory of Computing (1975), 66-71.

[11] Fortune, S., A note on sparse complete sets. SIAM Journal on Computing 8(1979), 431-433.

[12] Garey, M. and Johnson, D., Computers and intractability: a guide to the theory of NP-completeness. San Francisco: W.H. Freeman (1979).

[13] Gill, J., Computational complexity of probabilistic Turing machines. SIAM Journal on Computing 6(1977), 675-695.

[14] Hartmanis, J., On log-tape isomorphisms of complete sets. Theoretical Computer Science 7(1978), 273-286.

[15] Hartmanis, J. and Mahaney, S., An essay about research on sparse NP-complete sets. Proceedings of the 9th Symposium on Mathematical Foundations of Computer Science, Lecture Notes in Computer Science 88(1980), 40-57. Also Technical Report TR 80-244, Department of Computer Science, Cornell University (1980).

[16] Hartmanis, J. and Mahaney, S., On census complexity and sparseness of NP-complete sets. Technical Report TR 80-416, Department of Computer Science, Cornell University (April 1980).

[17] Hartmanis, J., Sewelson, V., and Immerman, N., Sparse sets in NP-P: EXPTIME versus NEXPTIME. Proceedings of the 15th ACM Symposium on Theory of Computing (1983), 382-391.

[18] Heller, H., On relativized exponential and probabilistic complexity classes. Information and Control, to appear.

[19] Hopcroft, J. and Ullman, J., Introduction to automata theory, languages, and computation. Reading, Mass.: Addison-Wesley (1979).

[20] Immerman, N. and Mahaney, S., Oracles for which NP has polynomial size circuits. Presented at the Conference on Computational Complexity Theory, University of California at Santa Barbara (March 1983).

[21] Johnson, D., The NP-completeness column: an ongoing guide. Journal of Algorithms (1981-present).

[22] Johnson, D.S., Demers, A., Ullman, J.D., Garey, M.R., and Graham, R.L., Worst case performance bounds for simple one-dimensional packing algorithms. SIAM Journal on Computing 3(1974), 299-325.

[23] Kannan, R., A circuit-size lower bound. Proceedings of the 22nd IEEE Symposium on Foundations of Computer Science (1981), 304-309.

[24] Karp, R., Reducibility among combinatorial problems. Complexity of computer computations (R.E. Miller and J.W. Thatcher, editors), New York: Plenum (1972), 85-103.

[25] Karp, R. and Lipton, R., Some connections between non-uniform and uniform complexity classes. Proceedings of the 12th ACM Symposium on Theory of Computing (1980), 302-309. Also as Turing machines that take advice, L'Ensignement Mathématique 28(1982), 191-210.

[26] Kurtz, S., On sparse sets in NP-P: relativizations. SIAM Journal on Computing 14(1985), 113-119.

[27] Kurtz, S., personal communication.

[28] Ladner, R., On the structure of polynomial time reducibility. Journal of the Association for Computing Machinery 22(1975), 155-171.

[29] Landweber, L.H., Lipton, R.J., and Robertson, E.L., On the structure of sets in NP and other complexity classes. Theoretical Computer Science 15(1981), 181-200.

[30] Long, T., A note on sparse oracles for NP. Journal of Computer and System Sciences 24(1982), 224-232.

[31] Long, T. and Selman, A., Relativizing complexity classes with sparse oracles. Journal of the Association for Computing Machinery, to appear.

[32] Mahaney, S., Sparse complete sets for NP: solution of a conjecture of Berman and Hartmanis. Proceedings of the 21st IEEE Symposium on Foundations of Computer Science (1980), 54-60. Final version in Journal of Computer and System Sciences 25(1982), 130-143.

[33] Mahaney, S., Feasibly computable equivalence relations on NP and co-NP. Presented at Conference on Recursion Theoretic Aspects of Computer Science, Purdue University (May 1981).

[34] Mahaney, S., On the number of p-isomorphism classes of NP-complete sets. Proceedings of the 22nd IEEE Symposium on Foundations of Computer Science (1981), 130-143.

[35] Mahaney, S., Sparse NP-complete sets. Ph.D. thesis, Cornell University (1981).

[36] Mahaney, S. and Simon, J., Polynomial self-reducibility and sparseness. Manuscript (1981).

[37] Mahaney, S. and Young, P., Reductions among polynomial isomorphism types. Theoretical Computer Science (1985), to appear.

[38] Meyer, A. and Paterson, M., With what frequency are apparently intractable problems difficult? Technical Report, Massachusetts Institute of Technology (February 1979).

[39] Meyer, A. and Stockmeyer, L., The equivalence problem for regular expressions with squaring requires exponential time. Proceedings of the 13th IEEE Symposium on Switching and Automata Theory (1972), 125-129.

[40] Pippenger, N., On simultaneous resource bounds. Proceedings of the 20th IEEE Symposium on Foundations of Computer Science (1979), 307-311.

[41] Post, E., Recursively enumerable sets of positive integers and their decision problems. Bulletin of the American Mathematical Society 50(1944), 284-316.

[42] Rabin, M., Probabilistic algorithms. Algorithms and Complexity (J.F. Traub, editor), New York: Academic Press (1976), 21-39.

[43] Simon, J., On some central problems in computational complexity. Technical Report TR 75-224, Cornell University (1975).

[44] Simon, J., On the difference between one and many. Proceedings of the 4th International Colloquium on Automata, Languages, and Programming, Lecture Notes in Computer Science (52), 480-491.

[45] Simon, J., A note on sparse sets and probabilistic polynomial time. Technical Report TR CS-80-13, Department of Computer Science, Pennsylvania State University (May 1980).

[46] Sipser, M., A complexity theoretic approach to randomness. Proceedings of the 15th ACM Symposium on Theory of Computing (1983), 330-335.

[47] Solovay, R., and Strassen, V., A fast Monte-Carlo test for primality. SIAM Journal on Computing 6(1977), 84-85.

[48] Stockmeyer, L, The polynomial time hierarchy. Theoretical Computer Science 3(1976), 1-22.

[49] Ukkonen, E., Two results on polynomial time turing reductions to sparse sets. Technical Report TR UCB/ERL M81/68, University of California at Berkeley (September 1981). Final version in SIAM Journal on Computing 12(1983), 580-587.

[50] Valiant, L., On the complexity of computing the permanent. Theoretical Computer Science 8(1979), 189-202.

[51] Wilson, C., Relativized circuit complexity. Proceedings of the 24th IEEE Symposium on Foundations of Computer Science (1983), 329-334.

[52] Yap, C., Some consequences of non-uniform conditions on uniform classes. Theoretical Computer Science 26(1983), 287-300.

[53] Yesha, Y., On certain polynomial-time truth-table reducibilities of complete sets to sparse sets. Technical Report, University of Toronto (1981). Final version in SIAM Journal on Computing 12(1983), 411-425.

Stephen R. Mahaney
AT&T Bell Laboratories
600 Mountain Avenue
Murray Hill, New Jersey 07974, U.S.A.

KENNETH McALOON
Models of arithmetic and complexity theory

1. INTRODUCTION

The study of models of arithmetic goes back to work of Gödel
and Skolem: there are non-standard structures which satisfy
the first-order Peano axioms. These structures prove to be
remarkably complex, and an elaborate set of methods for
studying them has been developed.

This subject has been particularly enhanced by the break-
through of Paris-Harrington-Kirby giving a finite combinatorial version of Gödel's Incompleteness Theorem as well as a
model-theoretic proof of the theorem. Complexity Theory is
the study of models of computation which takes into account
the utilization of resources such as time and space. Gödel's
technique of "arithmetization" established the connection
between arithmetic statements and computability; further work
by Church, Kleene and Turing refined and developed this connection. The purpose of this paper is to outline how certain
techniques and results of Models of Arithmetic are relevant to
problems in Complexity Theory and vice-versa.

We shall concentrate on two areas of research--initial
segments of Models of Arithmetic and the alternating linear
time hierarchy. The first deals with the complexity class of
the primitive recursive functions and relations and makes
extensive use of techniques introduced by Kirby and Paris

such as "regular initial segments"; the second is treated in
Section 4 and will exploit "bridging theorems" of Bennett,
Wrathall and others to link up the Model Theory and the
Complexity Theory.

The prerequisites for reading this paper are the elements
of Computability Theory (Turing machines, arithmetization,
primitive recursive functions) and the elements of Model
Theory (the first-order predicate calculus and the compactness
and completeness theorem). Section 2 reviews classical
material and serves as an introduction both to Section 3 and
Section 4; the latter two sections are for all practical
purposes independent of one another.

2. BACKGROUND MATERIAL

To discuss questions of definability in arithmetic and to
develop formal theories of arithmetic, we introduce a first-
order language appropriately called the language of arithmetic.
This language, denoted $\mathbb{L}$, consists of a constant symbol $\underset{\sim}{0}$,
a unary function symbol $\underset{\sim}{S}$ (for successor), binary function
symbols $\underset{\sim}{+}$ and $\underset{\sim}{\times}$, and a binary relation $\underset{\sim}{<}$; the language
also has equality, $\underset{\sim}{=}$, and an infinite list of variables
v_1, v_2, v_3, ... For legibility we shall use x, y, z, ...
as typical variables. We use $\underset{\sim}{1}$ to abbreviate $\underset{\sim}{S}\underset{\sim}{0}$, $\underset{\sim}{2}$ to
abbreviate $\underset{\sim}{SS0}$, and so on. In anticipation of our inter-
pretation of this language, we also write $x+1$ for $\underset{\sim}{S}x$,
$\underset{\sim}{x+2}$ for $\underset{\sim}{SS}x$, and so on. By a term of $\mathbb{L}$ we mean a polynomial P(x,y,z,...) where the x, y, z are variables of
the language and where the coefficients are underscored

120

natural numbers. A polynomial with no variables, such as $7 \times (3+5)$, is called a <u>closed</u> <u>term</u>.

The atomic formulas of the language are of two kinds:

equality of polynomials

$$P(x,y,z,\ldots) = Q(x,y,z,\ldots),$$

inequality of polynomials

$$P(x,y,z,\ldots) \leq Q(x,y,z,\ldots).$$

Further formulas are generated by Boolean connectives and existential quantification: $F \vee G$, $\neg F$ and $\exists xF$ are formulas if F and G are. The other Boolean connectives and the universal quantifier are considered abbreviations.

We denote the set of non-negative integers by $\mathbb{N}$. The set $\mathbb{N}$ together with the operations of successor, addition and multiplication and the order relation provide an interpretation for the language $\mathbb{L}$; quantifiers are interpreted as ranging over the non-negative integers. Thus if F is a formula of $\mathbb{L}$ without free variables, then either F holds in the model $\mathbb{N}$ or its negation $\neg F$ holds in $\mathbb{N}$; if F holds in $\mathbb{N}$, we write $\mathbb{N} \models F$. Thus we have

$$N \models \forall y \exists x \ (x > y \ \& \ \forall z \ (z \leq x \rightarrow z = 0 \vee z = 1$$
$$\vee \ \neg \exists u \ (u \leq x \ \& \ u \times z = x)))$$

which is the statement that there are infinitely many primes.
The fact that

$$\mathbb{N} \models \forall x \exists y \exists z \exists u \exists w \; [x = y{\times}y + z{\times}z + u{\times}u + w{\times}w]$$

is a result due to Lagrange. As two examples of statements about $\mathbb{N}$ that can be expressed in $\mathbb{L}$ and which hold in $\mathbb{N}$, we have the recursion equations for addition and multiplication:

$$\mathbb{N} \models \forall x \; (x + 0 = x) \; \& \; \forall x \, \forall y \; (x + Sy = S(x + y))$$
$$\mathbb{N} \models \forall x \; (x{\times}0 = 0) \; \& \; \forall x \, \forall y \; (x{\times}Sy = x{\times}y + y). \qquad (*)$$

The set of all closed formulas satisfied in $\mathbb{N}$ is called the <u>theory</u> <u>of</u> <u>True</u> <u>Arithmetic</u> which is abbreviated TA. The theory TA is a complete theory since every closed formula of $\mathbb{L}$ either holds in $\mathbb{N}$ or its negation holds in $\mathbb{N}$.

If a formula F has free variables, say $x_1, \ldots, x_k$, we write $F = F(x_1, \ldots, x_k)$. In this case, $F(x_1, \ldots, x_k)$ is neither true nor false in $\mathbb{N}$, but instead defines a subset of $\mathbb{N}^k$ consisting of those k-tuples $(n_1, \ldots, n_k)$ such that

$$\mathbb{N} \models F(n_1, \ldots, n_k)$$

where $F(n_1, \ldots, n_k)$ is the result of substituting the terms $n_1, \ldots, n_k$ for the variables $x_1, \ldots, x_k$. For example, the formula $F(x) \Longleftrightarrow \exists y \; (y{\times}y = x)$ defines the set of perfect squares and the formula $E(x,y,z) \Longleftrightarrow x{\times}y = z$ defines the graph of multiplication. A relation on $\mathbb{N}^k$ which is definable by a formula of $\mathbb{L}$ is <u>arithmetic</u> and is said to be arithmetically definable.

We now turn to other models of arithmetic. In general, a model or structure for the language of arithmetic is given by a set M together with a designated zero element 0_M, functions to interpret successor, plus and times and a binary relation to interpret the less-than predicate. So the model is given by a six-tuple $\langle M, 0_M, S_M, +_M, \times_M, <_M \rangle$. Throughout this paper, model will mean countable model and the set M will be a countable or denumerable set.

In order to define satisfaction and truth in general models M, it is first necessary to define the values of the polynomials with coefficients from M. Technically, we first define a valuation function for terms whose variables are assigned elements of M: if t is a term with free variables $x_1, \ldots, x_k$, then the value of t when x_1 is assigned $a_1, \ldots,$ and x_k is assigned a_k is denoted $t(a_1, \ldots, a_k)$ and is defined inductively by means of the clauses

$$\underset{\sim}{0}(a_1, \ldots, a_k) = 0_M$$
$$v_i(a_1, \ldots, a_k) = a_i$$
$$(\underset{\sim}{S}t)(a_1, \ldots, a_k) = S_M(t(a_1, \ldots, a_k))$$
$$(t_1 \underset{\sim}{+} t_2)(a_1, \ldots, a_k) = t_1(a_1, \ldots, a_k) +_M t_2(a_1, \ldots, a_k)$$
$$t_1 \underset{\sim}{\times} t_2(a_1, \ldots, a_k) = t_1(a_1, \ldots, a_k) \times_M t_2(a_1, \ldots, a_k).$$

Next, using the Tarski truth definitions, the satisfaction relation

$$M \models F(a_1, \ldots, a_k)$$

is defined by induction on the structure of the formula $F = F(x_1, \ldots, x_k)$. The meaning of $M \models F(a_1, \ldots, a_k)$ is "$F(x_1, \ldots, x_k)$ is true in M if x_1 is given the value a_1, x_2 the value a_2, $\ldots$, and x_k the value a_k." The relevant inductive clauses are

$$M \models (t_1 \simeq t_2)(a_1, \ldots, a_k) \iff$$
$$t_1(a_1, \ldots, a_k) = t_2(a_1, \ldots, a_k);$$

$$M \models (t_1 \lesssim t_2)(a_1, \ldots, a_k) \iff$$
$$t_1(a_1, \ldots, a_k) <_M t_2(a_1, \ldots, a_k);$$

$$M \models (F_1 \vee F_2)(a_1, \ldots, a_k) \iff$$
$$M \models F_1(a_1, \ldots, a_k) \text{ or } M \models F_2(a_1, \ldots, a_k);$$

$$M \models \neg F(a_1, \ldots, a_k) \iff \text{not}(M \models F(a_1, \ldots, a_k));$$

$$M \models \exists x F(x, a_1, \ldots, a_k) \iff$$
$$\text{for some } a \text{ in } M, \ M \models F(a, a_1, \ldots, a_k).$$

In the case of the model $\mathbb{N}$, we have

$$\mathbb{N} \models F(n_1, \ldots, n_k) \iff \mathbb{N} \models F(\underset{\sim}{n}_1, \ldots, \underset{\sim}{n}_k).$$

We noted above some sentences of the language of arithmetic which are satisfied in the structure $\mathbb{N}$ such as the recursion equations for plus and times (*). Another example is the Scheme of Mathematical Induction:

$$[F(\underset{\sim}{0},x_1,\ldots,x_n) \ \& \ \forall \ y[F(y,x_1,\ldots,x_n \rightarrow$$
$$F(Sy,x_1,\ldots,x_n)]] \rightarrow \ \forall xF(x,x_1,\ldots,x_n). \qquad (**)$$

For readability we have left out the initial universal
quantifiers $\forall x_1 \ldots \forall x_n$. Each choice of variable x and
choice of formula F of $\mathbb{L}$ determines an instance of the
mathematical induction scheme (**) and each such instance is
satisfied in $\mathbb{N}$ and so is a theorem of TA. There is a dual
scheme to (**) known as the <u>Least Element Principle</u>:

$$\exists \ xE(x,x_1,\ldots,x_n) \ \rightarrow \ \exists x[E(x,x_1,\ldots,x_n) \ \&$$
$$\forall \ y \ (y \underset{\sim}{\leq} x \ \rightarrow \ \neg E(y,x_1,\ldots,x_n)]. \qquad (***)$$

The duality between the schemes is the fact that mathematical
induction for F yields the Least Element Princple for $\neg$ F
and vice-versa.

   In the language $\mathbb{L}$ it is straightforward to express the
fact that $\underset{\sim}{<}$ is a total discrete order. The theory TA
includes statements that describe $\mathbb{N}$ as the non-negative part
of a commutative discretely ordered ring which also satisfies
the schemes (*), (**) and (***). The question was raised
whether $\mathbb{N}$ could be characterized up to isomorphism as the
ordered semi-ring which satisfies TA. This was shown not to
be the case by Skolem, using what one would call today an
ultrapower construction, [71]. This result can also be
obtained by application of the Compactness Theory of first-
order logic: let c be a new individual constant; consider

125

the set of formulas

$$\text{TA}, \quad c \neq 0, \quad c \neq 1, \quad \ldots, \quad c \neq n, \quad \ldots \; .$$

Each finite subset of this list of formulas has a model, namely $\mathbb{N}$ itself where the constant c is interpreted by a sufficiently large integer. Let M be a (countable) model of this set of formulas. Then in M, c is interpreted by an infinite integer and M is not isomorphic to $\mathbb{N}$. Models of TA which are not isomorphic to $\mathbb{N}$ are called non-standard. Note that non-standard models of TA have successor, addition and multiplication operations which continue to satisfy the recursion equations (*); the schemes of mathematical induction and Least Element Principle also continue to hold.

If a model M together with its functions and relations is a non-standard model of TA, the relation $<_M$ must be a total discrete ordering on M since the order axioms are expressible in a first-order way. The order relation on a non-standard model is rather easy to describe. All non-standard models begin with a copy of $\mathbb{N}$ itself and, in fact, the operations on M coincide with those of $\mathbb{N}$ on this initial segment; this is because

$$M \models \forall x \; (x < m \rightarrow x = 0 \vee x = 1 \vee \ldots \vee x = m - 1)$$

and because the equations and inequations that describe the graphs of the operations and the order relation on elements of

126

$\mathbb{N}$, such as $2 + 2 = 4$ and $3 < 5$, are all theorems of TA.
The infinite elements of a non-standard model are elements a
such that $M \models a \geq n$, for all n in the standard initial
part of the model. Each infinite or non-standard element a
of a model is surrounded by its "finitely close" neighbors:

$$... < a-2 < a-1 < a < a+1 < a+2 < ...$$

where we have dropped the subscript M for readability.
These elements form a strip ordered like the integers; let us
call this strip Z_a to suggest the order isomorphism with the
integers $\mathbb{Z}$. Let a and b be infinite integers in the
model M such that a < b (more precisely such that $a <_M b$).
Then either a is a finite distance from b and the two
elements lie on the same Z strip, that is $Z_a = Z_b$, or the
two are infinitely far apart and their Z strips are disjoint.
In the second case $Z_a < Z_b$ in the sense that $a + m < b - n$
for all finite integers m, n. Moreover, if $Z_a < Z_b$, then
there is another Z strip between these, namely $Z_{(a+b)/2}$ or
$Z_{(a+b+1)/2}$ when a + b is odd; to check this, suppose a+n <
b for all standard n. If $(a+b)/2 = a \pm k$ for some
standard k, then $a + b = 2a \pm 2k$ and $b = a \pm 2k$ which is
impossible since 2k is standard. So if $Z_a < Z_b$, then
$Z_a < Z_{(a+b)/2}$ and similarly $Z_{(a+b)/2} < Z_b$. So the Z
strips determined by the non-standard elements form a countable densely ordered set without first or last element; hence
their order type is that of rationals. So a picture of the

order structure of a non-standard model of TA would be as in
Figure 1.

$$\xrightarrow{\hspace{2cm}} \ldots \xleftarrow{\hspace{1cm}}\xrightarrow{\hspace{0.5cm}} \ldots \xleftarrow{\hspace{1cm}}\xrightarrow{\hspace{0.5cm}} \ldots \xleftarrow{\hspace{1cm}}\xrightarrow{\hspace{0.5cm}} \ldots \xleftarrow{\hspace{1cm}}\xrightarrow{\hspace{0.5cm}} \ldots$$

$\quad\quad$ ℕ $\quad\quad\quad\quad\quad\quad$ Z strips ordered like ℚ

Figure 1

Although the order structure of a non-standard model of TA
is easily described, the addition and multiplication tables
cannot be described at all; in recursion theoretic terms, what
we mean by this is that if the domain of the countable non-
standard model is identified with ℕ itself, then neither the
addition operation $+_M$ nor the multiplication operation $\times_M$
can be recursive or even arithmetically definable. This
result is due to Tennenbaum [77].

The link between definability in terms of the language of
arithmetic and computability was established by the method of
arithmetization introduced by Gödel in his 1931 paper [22].
In this watershed work, Gödel showed that all primitive recursive functions are definable in arithmetic in the following
sense: to each primitive recursive function $y = f(x)$ there
corresponds a formula $F(x,y)$ of the language 𝕃 which
satisfies

$$f(n) = m \iff \mathbb{N} \models F(n,m)$$

for all m, n in ℕ. The key to this representation is the

128

coding of a sequence of numbers by means of a single number
and a deciding in terms of addition and multiplication.
Recall that in the usual development of the machinery of the
primitive recursive functions, for example as in [41] or [24],
one shows that the function $n \rightarrow p_n$, the nth prime, is
primitive recursive. Then one maps the sequence $(k_1, \ldots, k_n)$
to the number $s = 2^{k_1} \ldots p_n^{k_n}$; the sequence number s is
then decoded in terms of exponentiation. However, in theories
of arithmetic based on successor, plus and times, some "diophantine" machinery is necessary first to express sequence
numbers and decoding before the development of exponentiation,
the list of primes and the other primitive recursive functions.
The method of Gödel is to define a sequence s in terms of a
triple of numbers a, b, c such that a is the length of the
sequence and b, c play the following roles: for $i < a$,
the numbers $b(i+1) + 1$ are to be relatively prime and the
i^{th} element of the sequence is the remainder when c is
divided by $b(i+1) + 1$. Given a sequence of a elements
bounded by n, one can take b such that $b > a$ and $b > n!$
and then find c by means of the Chinese Remainder Theorem.
The sequence number s is set to be the ordered triple
$\langle a,b,c \rangle$; the triple $\langle a,b,c \rangle$ can be defined in terms of a
pairing function such as $\langle x,y \rangle = [(x+y)(x+y+1)]/2 + y$. So
given $s = \langle a,b,c \rangle$ and $i < a$, the remainder of the division
$c/[b(i+1) + 1]$ will be denoted $(s)_i$.

   We need to examine more closely the arithmetic definitions
of the primitive recursive functions. To that end we

introduce two abbreviations:

$$\exists\, x{<}y \ \ F \quad \text{for} \quad \exists\, x \ (x \leq y \ \& \ F)$$
$$\forall\, x{<}y \ \ F \quad \text{for} \quad \forall\, x \ (x \leq y \ \rightarrow \ F).$$

When quantifiers appear in this context they are called bounded quantifiers. The class of bounded quantifier formulas of $\mathbb{L}$ is defined to be the smallest class containing the atomic formulas and closed under Boolean operations and bounded quantification. The bounded quantifier formulas are also called the Δ_0-formulas or Σ_0-formulas. As an example, consider the formula defining the class of prime numbers:

$$P(x) \ <\!\!=\!\!\!=\!\!> \ x \geq 1 \ \& \ \forall\, z{<}x \ \forall\, u{<}x \ (u \times z \neq x)$$

Another example is the decoding of a sequence number:

$$x = (s)_i \ <\!\!=\!\!\!=\!\!> \ \exists\, a,b,c{<}s \ [s = \langle a,b,c \rangle \ \& \ i < a \ \&$$
$$\exists\, q{<}s \ (c = ((i{+}1) \times b + 1) \times q + x)].$$

A formula is called Σ_1 if it is of the form

$$\exists\, xE$$

where E is a Δ_0-formula. Notice that if $\exists\, xE$ is a Σ_1-formula, then so is $\exists\, y\, \exists\, xE$ in the sense that we have the equivalence

130

$$\exists x \exists y E \longleftrightarrow \exists z \ ((\exists x<z)(\exists y<z) \ E).$$

It is also easy to check that conjunctions and disjunctions of Σ_1-formulas are also equivalent to Σ_1-formulas. By way of example consider

$$E(x,y) \Longleftrightarrow \exists s \ [s = \{a,b,c\} \ \& \ (s)_0 = 1 \ \&$$
$$\forall i \le a \ ((s)_{i+1} = 2 \times (s)_i \ \& \ x \le a \ \& \ (s)_x = y].$$

The abbreviations we have used all involve only bounded quantifiers; so $E(x,y)$ is a Σ_1-formula that defines the function $y = 2^x$.

The classical results linking definability in $\mathbb{N}$ and computability can be summarized as follows. To each Turing machine M, there corresponds a number e which codes M; there is a primitive recursive predicate $T(x,y,z)$, called the Kleene T-predicate, which encodes the relation between a machine, its input and the computation performed. A bit more precisely, when M is given the binary representation of the number n as its input, then $T(e,n,m)$ holds if M halts and if m is a code for the sequence of computation steps made by M. The T-predicate thus links machine computation on strings with primitive recursion on numbers. The next link in the chain is between primitive recursion and definability in the structure $\mathbb{N}$ by means of Σ_1-formulas of the language $\mathbb{L}$. This is a more precise statement of the aforementioned result of Gödel.

<u>Theorem 2.1.</u> The primitive recursive functions and relations
are Σ_1-definable in $\mathbb{N}$.

Thus the T-predicate is a Σ_1-subset of $\mathbb{N}^3$. Moreover,
for a Turing machine M with Gödel number e, the set of
natural numbers (whose string representations are) accepted by
M is defined in $\mathbb{N}$ by the Σ_1-formula $\exists y T(\underset{\sim}{e},x,y)$. Therefore, all recursively enumerable sets of integers are Σ_1-
definable. This also means that general recursive functions
can be defined in arithmetic in a standard way. There is a
primitive recursive function $z = U(y)$ whose "job" is to
decode the output value of a function from the "history of its
computation" y. That is, U has the following properties.
Let $f : \mathbb{N} \longrightarrow \mathbb{N}$ be a total function which is computed by
Turing machine M with code e. Then

$$z = f(x) \Longleftrightarrow \exists y [T(e,x,y) \ \& \ z = U(y)].$$

Thus the functional relation $z = f(x)$ is expressible in
arithmetic in a Σ_1-way, as is easily seen by combining
quantifiers.

To summarize, if $f : \mathbb{N} \longrightarrow \mathbb{N}$ is a computable total function, then there is a Δ_0-formula $G_f(x,y,z)$ of the language
$\mathbb{L}$ such that

$$n = f(m) \Longleftrightarrow \mathbb{N} \models \exists y G_f(m,y,n).$$

132

Because the computable functions can be expressed arithmetically via the T-predicate, they extend automatically to
all models of the theory TA. Thus if $f : \mathbb{N} \to \mathbb{N}$ is computable and is defined in $\mathbb{N}$ by means of the Δ_0-formula
$G_f(x,y,z)$, we extend f to a non-standard model M of TA
by setting

$$f_M(a) = b \iff M \models \exists y G_f(a,y,b)$$

for all elements a, b of the model M. Note that for
standard m, n we have

$$f(m) = n \iff \mathbb{N} \models \exists y G_f(m,y,n) \iff$$
$$M \models \exists y G_f(m,y,n) \iff f_M(m) = n.$$

As a consequence, non-standard models of TA inherit exponentiation, the enumeration of the primes and all the other
recursive functions; moreover, the primitive recursive
functions continue to satisfy their recursion equations. For
example, consider the case of exponentiation. Let the
function $x^y = z$ be defined in $\mathbb{N}$ by the Σ_1-formula
$E(x,y,z)$ and let us write $e(x,y) = z$ for $x^y = z$. Then for
non-standard M,

$$M \models \forall x E(x,\underset{\sim}{0},\underset{\sim}{1}) \ \& \ \forall x, y, z, w \ [(E(x,y,z) \ \&$$
$$E(x,y,w) \to w \underset{\sim}{=} z) \ \& \ (E(x,y,z) \to E(x,Sy,z \times x))].$$

133

In other symbols,

$$e_M(x, 0_M) = 1_M \qquad e_M(x, y +_M 1) = e_M(x,y) \times_M x.$$

This also means that the defining equations (*) for addition and multiplication hold in non-standard models of TA and that the coding machinery for finite sequences is available.

   If M is a non-standard model of TA, then M is totally ordered by the relation $<_M$. By an <u>initial</u> <u>segment</u> of M we mean a subset of M which is an initial segment of M considered as an ordered set. If I is such a subset, we write I < M. We extend this notation further and we write a < I if a is an element of the initial segment I.

   An important field of research on models of arithmetic is the analysis of the distribution of initial segments I < M which are closed under various operations of M. We will next look at initial segments closed under multiplication; later we shall consider initial segments closed under more powerful operations such as the primitive recursive functions.

   The first thing to remark about closure under multiplication is that if I < M is closed under the multiplication of M, then I must be closed under the addition of M. To see this, note that for b greater than 1, a+b < ab; so if a, b are elements of the initial segment I, the fact that ab < I implies a+b < I since I is an initial segment of M. By the same token, for an initial segment I < M to be closed under multiplication it is sufficient that it be closed under squaring. Let us remark that if I is closed under multiplication, then I itself is a structure for the language $\mathbb{L}$ of arithmetic with the induced functions and relations of M.

Backing up a step, let us describe a way of obtaining initial segments closed under successor and addition. So let M be a non-standard model and let a be an infinite integer of M. As above, a determines its strip Z_a. Let I consist of all integers on or below this strip. Thus $I = \{x : x < a+n,$ for some standard $n\}$. So I is closed under successor, but not under addition since $a+a > a+n$ for standard n. So $I < a+a < M$. The next initial segment we consider is $J = \{x : x < an,$ for some standard $n\}$. So J is closed under addition but J is not closed under multiplication since $a^2 > an,$ for standard n. Thus $J < a^2 < M$. Finally to obtain a proper initial segment of M closed under multiplication, we need only take $K = \{x : x < a^n,$ for some standard $n\}$. This segment will be closed under multiplication since $a^n \cdot a^m = a^{n+m}$. Also K is a proper initial segment since $K < a^a < M$. The reader will note that if a is standard, then the segments I, J and K defined in this discussion all coincide with $\mathbb{N}$.

A key fact about non-standard models M of TA is that no proper initial segment closed under successor can be definable in M. To see this, suppose $I < M$ is defined by a formula

F(x) of 𝕃 with parameters from M; then applying the Least Element Principle to the formula $\neg F(x)$, we have a least element b in M - I. So I must be equal to the interval [0, b-1]. Thus, in particular, ℕ cannot be definable in non-standard M. This fact gives rise to the "overspill" principle: if $M \models F(n)$ for all standard n, then for some infinite a in M, we have $M \models \forall x \leq aF(x)$.

Using the universal T-predicate, it is a straightforward diagonal argument to show that the class of recursively enumerable sets of integers is not closed under complementation. This means that there are Σ_1-definable sets of integers whose complements are not definable by means of formulas of the same type. The class of formulas dual to the Σ_1-formulas is the class of Π_1-formulas: $\forall xE$, where E is a Δ_0-formula. Thus the class of sets definable by Π_1-formulas and the class of sets definable by Σ_1-formulas do not coincide.

Since sequence numbers permit set-theoretic operations in arithmetic, the language 𝕃 itself can be defined in terms of natural numbers. The set of formulas is then a recursive set and the usual syntactic operations on formulas such as taking disjunctions, negations and substituting for variables and terms are all recursive. The theory TA itself is then subject to recursion-theoretic analysis. It is a classical result that there is no recursive (even arithmetic) set of axioms for TA. Let us remark that this result follows from

136

the fact that recursively enumerable sets are definable in
arithmetic together with the fact that there exist recursively
enumerable non-recursive sets. To sketch this proof, let
$\exists y T(e,x,y)$ define a recursively enumerable non-recursive set
X. For each integer m, either $\exists y T(e,\underset{\sim}{m},y)$ or
$\neg \exists y T(e,\underset{\sim}{m},y)$ is an element of TA. So if TA had a recursive set of axioms, say AX, then by enumerating all
consequences of AX until either $\neg \exists y T(e,\underset{\sim}{m},y)$ or
$\exists y T(e,\underset{\sim}{m},y)$ appeared, one would have a recursive algorithm
for deciding membership in X. Since TA is a complete
theory, another way of phrasing this result is that TA
itself is not a recursively enumerable set. Hence any recursively enumerable subtheory of TA is necessarily incomplete; this is an alternative statement of the First
Incompleteness Theorem.

3.   INITIAL SEGMENTS OF MODELS OF ARITHMETIC

Recursively axiomatizable subtheories of TA are incomplete.
One task of Mathematical Logic has been to analyze this
phenomenon and to bring to light statements of TA which are
independent of important axiomatizable subtheories. Our goal

in this section is to outline the Kirby-Paris model-theoretic
methods which lead to a cogent analysis of the incompleteness
of certain theories in terms of the rate of growth of
recursive functions. The primitive recursive predicates and
functions are the complexity class of interest in this section,
and we will apply the methods developed to determine whether
various functions and decision procedures fall within this
complexity class.

We now introduce various axiom sets and subtheories of TA.
First we list the axioms for the basic operations of arithmetic. As is customary, we omit the universal quantifiers in
the statement of these axioms:

$$0 \neq Sx \qquad x \neq 0 \rightarrow \exists y (x = Sy)$$
$$Sx = Sy \rightarrow x = y$$
$$x + 0 = x \qquad x + Sy = S(x+y)$$
$$x \times 0 = 0 \qquad x \times Sy = x \times y + x.$$

This set of axioms forms a theory known as Q, cf. [76].
The key facts about Q are that a faithful copy of $\mathbb{N}$ is
included in all of its models and that it is an essentially
undecidable finitely axiomatizable theory; for definitions and
proofs, again cf. [76]. Adjoining the following axiom for
the less-than relation to Q yields a theory known as PA^-:

138

$$x \leq y \longleftrightarrow \exists u \ (u \neq 0 \ \& \ x+u = y).$$

Further theories are typically obtained by adding induction axioms to PA^- and making restrictions on the formulas in the induction scheme (**) above.

At this point we will stop belaboring the distinction between expressions and formulas in the formal language $\mathbb{L}$ and ordinary informal arithmetic usage. That is, we will drop the use of underscored symbols and also begin to use ordinary exponential notation and other current arithmetic abbreviations. We will also omit the subscript M when discussing plus, times and the order relation on integers in non-standard models. The aim is, of course, readability.

By Open Induction we mean the theory obtained by adjoining to PA^- those instances of the induction scheme (**) where the formula F is quantifier-free. Note that the Least Element Principle (***) for open formulas is derivable in Open Induction since the negation of an open formula is again open. Non-standard models of Open Induction have been explicitly constructed by Shepherdson [70]; his construction shows that the assertion $\exists x, y \ (x^2 = 2y^2)$ is consistent with Open Induction. This assertion contradicts the irrationality of the square root of 2.

By $I\Delta_0$ we mean the theory obtained by adjoining to PA^- those instances of the induction scheme (**) where F is restricted to be a bounded quantifier formula. Again note that the Least Element Principle for bounded quantifier formulas is provable in this theory. The theory $I\Delta_0$ is quite rich and a sizeable portion of elementary number theory can be formalized or "carried out" in this theory. Thus in $I\Delta_0$ it can be shown that plus and times are commutative, that the g.c.d. of two numbers exists, that $(a,b) = 1$ implies $ax = by + 1$ for some $x, y,$ and that the square root of 2 is irrational. It is an interesting open question whether the existence of unboundedly many primes can be proved in this theory, cf. [78]. Progress on this question has been made recently by Paris and Wilkie: using work of Woods [82], they have shown that the existence of unboundedly many primes can be proved in the theory $I\Delta_0 + \forall x \ (x^{(\log x)}$ exists$)$. Since $I\Delta_0$ is a recursively axiomatizable subtheory of TA, it is therefore incomplete by the First Incompleteness Theorem. But the consequences of $I\Delta_0$ in the sublanguage of $\mathbb{L}$ without multiplication coincide with complete Presburger Arithmetic and its consequences in the sublanguage without addition and less-than yield complete Skolem Arithmetic, cf. [8] and [9]. It is open whether $I\Delta_0$ is finitely axiomatizable; this question appears to be deep and is related to other "long-standing" problems.

In the discussion above, we showed that if M is a non-standard model of TA and if a is an integer of M, then

$$K = \{x : x < a^n, \text{ for some standard } n\}$$

is an initial segment of M which is closed under the

addition and multiplication of M. Since K is closed under $+_M$ and $\times_M$, K itself is a structure of the language of arithmetic $\mathbb{L}$. Since K < M, that is, since K is an initial segment of M, we can show that K is a model of $I\Delta_0$: suppose F(x) is a Δ_0-formula with parameters from K and that K $\models \exists x F(x)$. So for some b < K, K $\models$ F(b). The formula F(b) only has bounded quantifiers; since K is an initial segment of M, the bounded universal and existential quantifiers have the same scope in K as in M. So M $\models$ F(b). The Least Element Principle holds in M; so let c be the least element in M which satisfies F(x). We must have M $\models$ c $\leq$ b & F(c). So c < K and K $\models$ F(c) & $\forall$ x (x < c $\longrightarrow$ $\neg$F(x)).

Thus models of $I\Delta_0$ "abound" among the initial segments of non-standard models of TA. From the recursion-theoretic point of view, however, non-standard models of $I\Delta_0$ cannot be effectively presented. By this we mean that if the domain of a model of $I\Delta_0$ is identified with $\mathbb{N}$, the addition and multiplication of this model are both non-recursive, cf. [45]. In [78] it is shown that this also holds true of the subsystem of $I\Delta_0$ obtained by restricting induction to formulas in prenex form with no universal bounded quantifiers. For other results on the recursion-theoretic complexity of models of arithmetic, we refer the reader to [49].

The next theory we introduce is $I\Sigma_1$; this theory is axiomatized by PA^- together with the induction scheme (**) restricted to Σ_1-formulas. Thus $I\Sigma_1$ extends $I\Delta_0$. The remarks about the recursion-theoretic complexity of models of $I\Delta_0$ therefore apply to $I\Sigma_1$. Moreover, to develop a method of construction of proper initial segments $I < M$ which satisfy $I\Sigma_1$ is not an easy task. In fact, much of the remainder of this chapter will be devoted to the problem of determining the distribution of segments $I < M$ which satisfy $I\Sigma_1$.

Since $I\Sigma_1$ is axiomatized by the scheme of Mathematical Induction for Σ_1-formulas, this yields the Least Element Principle for Π_1-formulas by duality. However, the Least Element Principle for Σ_1-formulas requires a proof, which we now sketch.

Suppose $P(x)$ is a Σ_1-formula, that $P(a)$ holds, that $P(0)$ fails and that $\exists x (x < a \ \& \ P(x))$ also holds. To find the least c such that $P(c)$, we consider the predicate

$$B(x) \Longleftrightarrow x < a \ \& \ \exists y \ [x < y \leq a \ \& \ P(a-y)].$$

The predicate $B(x)$ is provably (in $I\Sigma_1$) equivalent to a Σ_1-predicate. By hypothesis, $B(0)$ holds since a is not the least solution to $P(x)$. So either $\forall x (B(x) \rightarrow B(x+1))$ or else $B(b) \ \& \ \neg B(b+1)$ holds for some b. The first alternative is impossible since, by Mathematical Induction, it implies $\forall x B(x)$ and, in particular, $B(a)$ which is false. So for some b, we have $B(b) \ \& \ \neg B(b+1)$. Clearly, $b+1 < a$ since $B(b) \ \& \ \neg P(0)$; equally clearly, if y satisfies $b+1 < y < a$, then $\neg P(a-y)$ holds. We claim $c = a - (b+1)$

142

is the least element satisfying $P(x)$. For if not, there would exist u such that $0 < u < a - (b+1)$ and $P(u)$; but then $a-u = d > b+1$ and $P(a-d)$ which contradicts $\neg B(b+1)$.

In effect, we have shown that $I\Pi_1$ is a subtheory of $I\Sigma_1$. Conversely, in a similar manner one shows that $I\Sigma_1$ is a subtheory of $I\Pi_1$ and thus the two theories are equivalent. So intuitively speaking, $I\Sigma_1$ is the theory of arithmetic which is based on the Least Number Principle for recursively enumerable sets and for complements of recursively enumerable sets. This is a powerful theory which captures a significant part of mathematical practice. As we shall see, it has the same proof-theoretic strength as Skolem's Primitive Recursive Arithmetic [72].

In order to capture the primitive recursive operations in $I\Sigma_1$, the appropriate amount of Gödel coding machinery must be set up. In $I\Sigma_1$ the following scheme can be proved, cf. [25]:

$$\forall x \exists y F(x,y,x_1,\ldots,x_n) \longrightarrow$$
$$\forall x \exists s \forall i < x F(i,(s)_i,x_1,\ldots,x_n), \quad \text{(iv)}$$
$$F \quad a \quad \Sigma_1\text{-formula.}$$

The scheme is first proved for F in Δ_0 and then extended to Σ_1-formulas by pairing existential quantifiers. With this scheme the primitive recursive functions can be introduced in $I\Sigma_1$ in the natural way; for example the exponential function $z = x^y$ can be defined by

$$z = x^y \iff (y = 0 \ \& \ z = 1) \lor (y > 0 \ \& \ \exists s \ (s)_0 = 1 \ \&$$
$$\forall i < y \ (s_{i+1} = (s)_i \cdot x \ \& \ (s)_y = z))$$

and by induction on y one proves

$$I\Sigma_1 \vdash \forall x \forall y \exists ! z \ (z = x^y).$$

Here $\exists ! z$ is an abbreviation for "there exists a unique z." Other primitive recursive functions are introduced by boot-strapping on previously introduced ones. Thus iterated exponentiation $z = x^{[y]}$ is defined in terms of exponenti-ation

$$z = x^{[y]} \iff (y = 0 \ \& \ z = 1) \lor (y > 0 \ \& \ \exists s \ ((s)_1 = x \ \&$$
$$\forall i < y \ (i > 0 \longrightarrow (s)_{i+1} = (s)_i^x \ \& \ (s)_y = z))$$

and we have $I\Sigma_1 \vdash \forall x \forall y \exists ! z \ (z = x^{[y]})$. Note also that by rearranging quantifiers, both $z = x^y$ and $z = x^{[y]}$ are Σ_1-definable in $I\Sigma_1$ just as in $\mathbb{N}$. This continues to hold up through the primitive recursive hierarchy.

The theory obtained by adding the full induction scheme (**) to PA^- is called Peano Arithmetic and is denoted PA. In this theory scheme (iv) is provable without any restriction on the formula F. The Least Element Principle is also prov-able for all formulas.

Remark. The scheme (iv) is crucial to proving the Second Incompleteness Theorem that consistency of a theory T is not

144

provable in T if T is sufficiently strong. In his paper
[22], Gödel gives an informal proof that the scheme is valid
in $\mathbb{N}$; since this informal proof can be formalized in
Principia Mathematica, the scheme is thus established for the
arithmetic of Principia Mathematica. From this the Second
Incompleteness Theorem is derived for Principia Mathematica
(and other set theories). Gödel remarks at the end of his
paper that his proof can be carried out directly in PA; the
first published proof of this is in [25].

Let T denote a subtheory of TA. Let $f : \mathbb{N} \longrightarrow \mathbb{N}$ be a
total recursive function. We say that f is a <u>provably</u>
<u>recursive</u> <u>function</u> of T iff for some Δ_0-formula $G_f(x,y,z)$
we have

(i) $T \vdash \forall x \exists !y \exists z G_f(x,y,z)$,

(ii) $m = f(n) \Longleftrightarrow \mathbb{N} \models \exists z G_f(n,m,z)$.

From our discussion so far we have the following result.

Theorem 3.1. Each of the following holds:

(i) Every polynomial function is a provably recursive
function of $I\Delta_0$.

(ii) Every primitive recursive function is a probably
recursive function of $I\Sigma_1$.

(iii) Every recursive total function is a probably recursive
function of TA.

Part (i) is trivial. Part (ii) follows from our discussion
of the bootstrapping procedure to define the primitive recursive functions in $I\Sigma_1$. Part (iii) follows from the existence
of the Kleene T-predicate and the fact that total recursive

functions are Σ_1-definable in $\mathbb{N}$. The situation for PA is analogous to that for $I\Sigma_1$; at the end of this section we state a result of Paris and Harrington [61] which character-izes the provably recursive functions of PA. Our task now is to develop converses to parts (i) and (ii). Our first result in this direction shows that provably recursive functions of $I\Delta_0$ cannot grow more rapidly than polynomial functions.

Theorem 3.2. Every provably recursive function of $I\Delta_0$ is bounded by a polynomial function.

Proof. This result, in somewhat sharper form, is due to Parikh [56]. We give a model-theoretic proof of the theorem as stated. Let g be a recursive function such that for every s in $\mathbb{N}$, $g(n) > n^s$ infinitely often. Suppose $I\Delta_0 \vdash \forall x \exists ! y \exists z G(x,y,z)$ and that $g(n) = m \iff \mathbb{N} \models \exists z G(n,m,z)$, where G is a Δ_0-formula. Let c be a new individual constant and let $g(c) > c^s$ be an abbreviation for $\exists y \exists z (G(c,y,z) \& y > c^s)$. Consider the set of closed formulas $TA \cup \{g(c) > c^s : s$ a standard integer$\}$. Every finite set of these formulas is consistent; in fact, given $s_1, \ldots, s_t$, the structure $\mathbb{N}$ itself is a model of TA, $g(c) > c^s, \ldots, g(c) > c^s$ where c is interpreted by an integer r at which $g(r) > r^m$ where $m = \max(s_i)$. By the Compactness Theorem, the infinite set of formulas has a model M. In M, c is (interpreted by) a non-standard integer. Let $b = g_M(c)$; that is, $M \models \exists z G(c,b,z)$. By construction, we must have $M \models c^s < b$, for all standard s. Now let

146

$K = \{a : M \models a < c^s, \text{ for some standard } s\}$. As before, K is a model of $I\Delta_0$ but $K < b$. We claim that K cannot satisfy $\forall x \exists ! y \exists z G(x,y,z)$, which will contradict the hypothesis that g was a provably recursive function of $I\Delta_0$. So suppose we did have $K \models G(c,b',d)$ for some $b', d < K$. Since G is Δ_0, we would also have $M \models G(c,b',d)$, yielding $b = b'$, which is impossible. $\square$

Let us consider some of the connections between provably recursive functions and initial segments. For example, suppose g is a provably recursive function of the theory T; then if M is a model of TA and if $I < M$ is a model of T, the initial segment I is closed under g_M and in fact g_I coincides with the restriction of g_M to I. Suppose further that f is a recursive function which is majorized by g. This means that we have

$$\mathbb{N} \models \forall x \forall y \forall y' \forall z \forall z' [G_g(x,y,z) \ \& \ G_f(x,y',z') \longrightarrow$$
$$y' \leq y].$$

This formula is Π_1 and a theorem of TA. So if $M \models$ TA and $I < M$ then I also satisfies this formula; therefore, if I is closed under g, then I is also closed under f. Later we will have a partial converse to this.

We now define a concept which will play a key role in the formulation of incompleteness theorems.

A sequence $\{f_n\}$ of recursive functions is said to be an <u>envelope</u> for the theory T if

(i) each f_n is a provably recursive function of T;

(ii) for all n, $f_n(x) \leq f_{n+1}(x)$;

(iii) whenever g is a provably recursive function of T, then for some n, g is majorized by f_n;

(iv) the function $F : (n,x) \longrightarrow f_n(x)$ is itself recursive.

So essentially an envelope for a theory is a recursive squence of provably recursive functions which majorize all the provably recursive functions of the theory; condition (ii) is a less crucial one that can be satisfied by means of a simple manipulation of a sequence satisfying the other conditions. The condition (iv), which assures that the sequence $\{f_n\}$ is recursive, means that the sequence itself extends from $\mathbb{N}$ to non-standard models of TA; so we will write $f_a(x)$ for $F(a,x)$ when a is non-standard as well as standard.

A first remark to make is that there can be no envelope for TA. For the diagonal function $x \longrightarrow f_n(n)$ would be provably recursive for TA but not majorized by any f_n. From Theorem 3.2 we see that the polynomial functons $x \longrightarrow x^n + n$ form an envelope for $I\Delta_0$. Another straightforward example is given by the theory $I\Delta_0$ + EXP, which is obtained by adding a binary function symbol exp for exponentiation to $\mathbb{L}$ and augmenting $I\Delta_0$ with the defining equations for exponentiation. Then the functions $f_{n+1}(x) = 2^{f_n(x)}$ form an envelope for $I\Delta_0$ + EXP. For more studied analysis of this theory, we refer the reader to [16], and [9].

The above remarks about $I\Delta_0$ and exponentiation can be extended to other functions in the primitive recursive

148

hierarchy. What is more of a challenge is to find envelopes for powerful theories such as $I\Sigma_1$ and PA. The following key result of Kirby and Paris [35] provides a tool for generating envelopes of theories.

Theorem 3.3. Let T be a subtheory of TA and let $\{f_n\}$ be a sequence of functions satisfying conditions (i), (ii) and (iv) above. Then $\{f_n\}$ is an envelope for T if and only if for every non-standard model M of TA, for every a in M and for every non-standard b in M, there exists I < M such that $a < I < f_b(a)$ and I is a model of T.

A proof of this theorem in generality requires the "game-theoretic indicators" of [35] and [32]. We will not develop this machinery in this discussion, although it is closely related to the concept of envelope for a theory. For further papers dealing with "game-theoretic indicators" we refer the reader to [34] and [45]. The Kirby-Paris result has striking corollaries.

Corollary 3.4. Let $\{f_n\}$ be an envelope for T. Then the statement $\forall x \exists y \, [y = f_x(x)]$ is not provable in T although for each standard k the statement $\forall x \exists y \, [y = f_k(x)]$ is provable in T. Moreover, if g is any recursive function which eventually majorizes every f_n then $\forall x \exists y \exists z G_g(x,y,z)$ is not provable in T.

Proof. Let M be a non-standard model of TA. Let a be an infinite integer in M and let I < M be a model of T such

149

that $a < I < f_a(a)$. Then I is a model of T but not of $\forall x \exists y\ [y = f_x(x)]$. For the second part, by a compactness argument obtain $M \models TA$ with non-standard c satisfying $M \models f_n(c) < g(c)$ for all standard n. By overspill, there is non-standard b such that $M \models f_b(c) < g(c)$. This yields $I \models T$ such that $c < I < g(c)$. $\square$

This corollary is an incompleteness theorem and the first example for arithmetic with a model-theoretic proof. There is, however, a connection with Gödel's Second Incompleteness Theorem. It has been shown, cf. [44,61], that for envelopes constructed in the standard ways the statement $\forall x \exists y\ [y = f_x(x)]$ is equivalent to a Gödel statement implying the consistency of T and, in fact, the 1-consistency of T.

The next corollary will lead to a useful method for determining bounds on the rate of growth of recursive functions.

Corollary 3.5. Let $\{f_n\}$ be an envelope for T and let f be a recursive function. Suppose that for every model M and for every $I < M$, if I is a model of T then I is closed under f. Then f is majorized by some f_n.

Proof. Suppose not. Consider the set of sentences $TA +$ $\{f(c) > f_n(c) : n\ \text{standard}\}$. Since f is assumed not to be majorized by any f_n and since the f_n satisfy the monotonicity conditions (ii) and (iii), this set of formulas is consistent and so has a non-standard model M in which c is (interpreted by) an infinite integer. By the theorem, there exists $I < M$ such that $c < I$ and $I \models T$ and $I < f(c)$.

150

But then I is not closed under f. □

We have seen that all the primitive recursive functions are provably recursive in $I\Sigma_1$; using these Kirby-Paris techniques we will develop the converse of this and obtain combinatorial incompleteness results for $I\Sigma_1$. This will thus yield examples of recursive functions defined through combinatorial results which grow faster than the primitive recursive functions.

So consider the following sequence of functions:

$$F_0(x) = 2x + 1$$
$$F_{n+1}(x) = F_n^{(x+2)}(x)$$

where

$$F_n^{(x+2)}(x) = F_n(F_n(\ldots (F_n(x)) \ldots))$$
$$\text{-- } (x+2) \text{ times -- .}$$

Each function F_n is primitive recursive. Every primitive recursive function is majorized by some function F_n in the sequence and the function of two variables $F(n,m) = F_n(m)$ is "essentially" Ackermann's function. Our goal is to show that $\{F_n\}$ is an envelope for $I\Sigma_1$; this will imply that the provably recursive functions of $I\Sigma_1$ are primitive recursive and thus that these two classes coincide.

An injective map $j : M \longrightarrow M'$ is called an <u>elementary</u> <u>embedding</u> if for all formulas $F(x_1,\ldots,x_n)$ and all

$a_1, \ldots, a_n$ in M, we have

$$M \models F(a_1, \ldots, a_n) \iff M' \models F(j(a_1), \ldots, j(a_n)).$$

By way of example, if M' is any model of TA, the canonical embedding of $\mathbb{N}$ as an initial segment of M' is elementary for the simple reason that for standard $k_1, \ldots, k_n$ the sentence $F(\underset{\sim}{k}_1, \ldots, \underset{\sim}{k}_n)$ is in TA if and only if it is satisfied in $\mathbb{N}$. Of course, if M' is not a model of full TA, then the canonical embedding of $\mathbb{N}$ into M' is not elementary.

It was shown by MacDowell and Specker [47] that for every model M of PA there is an extension M' and an elementary embedding $j : M \longrightarrow M'$ such that $j(M) < M'$; that is, so that the image $j(M)$ of M under j is an initial segment of M'. The picture is this:

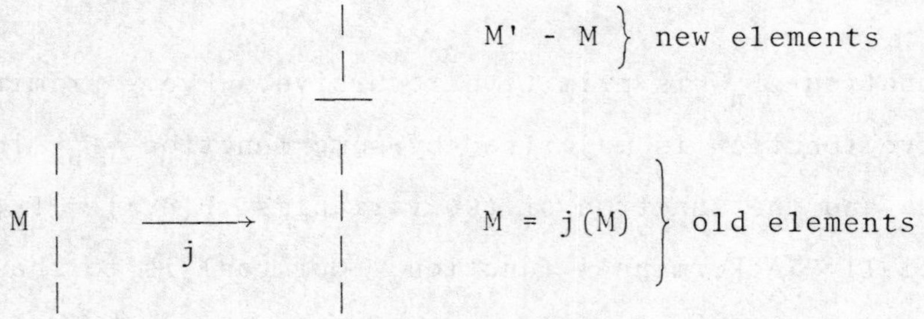

Figure 2

In fact this picture characterizes PA among extensions of
$I\Sigma_1$ (cf. [43,36]). Kirby and Paris, and independently Mills
[54], studied the conditions on I < M necessary to realize
the next picture. For our purposes we take M and M' to be
models of TA.

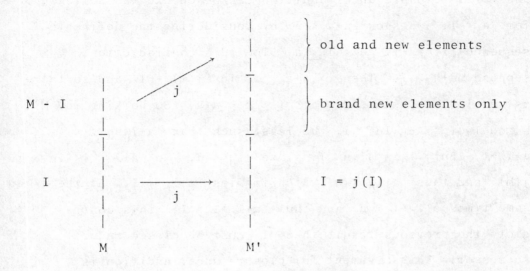

Figure 3

In this picture, j maps the initial segment I of M onto
an initial segment j(I) of M' and interpolates new non-
standard elements between j(I) and j(M-I). Note that the
first picture is a "special case" of the second. If I < M
is an initial segment for which there exists an elementary
embedding j which realizes Figure 3, then I is called a
regular initial segment or regular cut of M. Using a
compactness argument, one can check that the standard integers
ℕ form a regular initial segment of any non-standard model M.

153

Before turning to problems of the existence and distribution of regular initial segments, let us look at some closure properties they must satisfy. So suppose $I < M$ is regular. Since we have $j(I) = I$, I must be closed under successor: an elementary embedding cannot insert an integer between a and $a+1$. Closure under addition can be checked as follows: for $a < I$, we show $a+a < I$ by considering the definable sequence $x = a+i$, $0 \leq i \leq a$. Toward a contradiction, suppose $a+a > I$. Then $j(a+a)$ is in $j(M) - I$ and so there is c in M' such that $a < I < c < a+a$. So working in M', a model of TA, let i_0 be least such that $a+i_0 \leq c < a+i_0+1$. But i_0 is in I since $i_0 \leq a$. So $a+i_0$ is in $j(M)$ and thus $a+i_0 < c$ which implies $a+i_0 < I$. At the same time $a+i_0+1 > c$ and thus $a+i_0+1 > I$; this contradicts the previous result that I must be closed under successor. This argument for closure under addition is perfectly typical, and we can continue to bootstrap in this way to show I closed under multiplication, then exponentiation and so on through the sequence F_n. It follows that regular initial segments are closed under all primitive recursive functions.

Regular initial segments are thus seen to be closed under the primitive recursive functions. We can strengthen this further and show that regular initial segments must be models of the theory $I\Sigma_1$. To verify this assertion, suppose $F(x,y)$ is a Δ_0-formula with parameters from $I < M$, where I is regular, and suppose that $I \models \exists x \exists y F(x,y)$. Let $a < I$ be such that $I \models \exists y F(a,y)$. Let M', j be as in the picture and let c be such that $c < j(M-I)$ and $j(I) < c$. Consider the Δ_0-formula $H(x) \Longleftrightarrow x \leq a \ \& \ \exists y < c F(x,y)$. Let $b < M'$ be least such that $M' \models H(b)$. Then $b \leq a$ so $b < I$ and $I \models \forall x < b \forall y \neg F(x,y)$. However, $M' \models \exists y F(b,y)$ implies $M \models \exists y F(b,y)$. Therefore, there is in M a least y such that $M \models F(b,y)$. Finally, since $M' \models \exists y < c F(b,y)$ and since $M \models \forall y < y_0 \neg F(b,y)$, it follows that $y_0 < c$ and that $y_0 < I$ since $c < j(M-I)$. Hence, $I \models \exists y F(b,y)$ and $I \models \forall x < b \forall z \neg F(x,z)$.

Regular initial segments derive their name from a characterization which is analogous to a property of regular cardinals in set theory. The set-theoretic property is a variation of the pigeon-hole principle: if a large set is the union of a small number of sets, then one of them must be large. For the analogue of this in our context we first need a definition.

Let $I < M$ and let X be a subset of M; then X is said to be _unbounded_ in I if for every $a < I$ there is an integer b in $X \cap I$ such that $a < b$. A set which is not unbounded is called _bounded_. For a definable subset X of M, X is bounded in an initial segment I if and only if there are $a < I < b$ such that $X \cap [a,b]$ is empty; to verify this equivalence, note that the $\Longleftarrow$ direction is obvious. For the other direction, take $a < I$ such that $X \cap (I - a) = \emptyset$; then let b be the largest integer such that $X \cap [a,b] = \emptyset$.

The following theorem of [35] gives this "regular cardinal" characterization of regular initial segments.

Theorem 3.6. Let M be a model of PA and let I < M be an initial segment of M. Then the following conditions are equivalent:

(i)   I is a regular initial segment;

(ii)   for every a < I and every definable function
       F : M ⟶ M if M ⊨ ∀x [F(x) < a] then for some
       $i_0 < a$, the set $F^{-1}(i_0) = \{x : F(x) = i_0\}$ is
       unbounded in I.

For the proof we refer the reader to [35]. In the direction (ii) ⟹ (i) the proof uses an ultrapower argument in the spirit of the proof of the MacDowell-Specker result. In the other direction, if M, j and M' are as in Figure 3, given definable F : M ⟶ M' with F(x) < a < I, transport F to M', choose some newly interpolated point c, I < c < j(M) - I, and take $i_0 = F(c)$. Then $X = F^{-1}(i_0)$ is a definable subset of M; if X were bounded in I, there would be a < I < b in M such that M ⊨ X ∩ [a,b] = ∅. Hence M' ⊨ $F^{-1}(i_0)$ ∩ [a,b] = ∅, contradicting the choice of c.

To relate regular initial segments and closure under the functions F_n an intermediate class of initial segments must be brought in. We make a definition. Let M be a model of PA and let I < M be an initial segment; then I is said to be semi-regular if for any increasing definable function F : M ⟶ M' and any a < I, there is b < I such that

156

$x < a$ and $F(x) < I$ imply $F(x) < b$. This property of initial segments is the analogue of another property of regular cardinals in set theory: the supremum of a short sequence of small ordinals is small. In set theory (with the Axiom of Choice!) the properties that correspond to "regular" and "semi-regular" are equivalent, but this is not quite the case in models of arithmetic. Regular initial segments are easily seen to be semi-regular, but the converse fails, cf. [35]. Theorem 3.7 below will show that there is a partial converse, however.

The sequence $\{F_n\}$ leads to semi-regular initial segments in the following way. If $b < M$ is infinite, then for every a in M, if $M \models c = F_b(a)$ there is an initial segment I such that $a < I < c$ and I is semi-regular. The proof of this proceeds by constructing I in an infinite number of steps repeatedly using the following fact about the functions F_n: let $a = x_0 \leq x_1 \leq \ldots \leq x_a = F_{n+1}(a)$ be a sequence of length a going from a to $F_{n+1}(a)$; then for some $i' < a$, we have $F_n(x_{i'}) \leq x_{i'+1}$. Thus the interval $[x_i, x_{i'+1}]$ inherits the same property vis-á-vis F_{n-1}. If one starts with an interval $[a, F_b(a)]$ with b infinite, this process can be continued ad infinitum; for the full argument, cf. [35].

The last line of the argument shows that if there is an initial segment I such that $a < I < b$ and such that I is closed under the functions F_n for all standard n, then there is a semi-regular initial segment J satisfying $a < J < b$. Note, however, that closure under the F_n does

157

not imply semi-regularity. As an example, consider $I = \{x : x < F_n(a)$ for some standard $n\}$ and the definable sequence $s_i = F_i(a)$, $i \le a$.

As noted before, semi-regular initial segments are not necessarily regular; the partial converse is that if there is a semi-regular initial segment between a and b, then there is also a regular initial segment between a and b. This result, due to Harrington, uses a beautiful "finite Löwenheim-Skolem" argument and the Kirby-Paris method of indicators. A proof is given in [58]. The following theorem summarizes the situation.

Theorem 3.7. Let M be a non-standard model of TA and let $a < b$ be integers in M. Then the following are equivalent:

  (i)   there is a semi-regular I such that $a < I < b$;

 (ii)   there is regular I such that $a < I < b$;

(iii)   there is I such that $I \models I\Sigma_1$ and $a < I < b$;

 (iv)   there is I such that I is closed under the F_n for standard n and $a < I < b$;

  (v) $F_n(a) < b$ for all standard n;

 (vi) $F_c(a) < b$ for some infinite $c < M$.

This theorem has several corollaries.

Corollary 3.8. The sequence of functions $\{F_n\}$ forms an envelope for $I\Sigma_1$; thus the statement $\forall x \exists y \, [y = F_x(x)]$ is not provable in $I\Sigma_1$.

Corollary 3.9. A recursive function g is majorized by a primitive recursive function if and only if for all non-standard models M of TA and all regular initial segments I < M, I is closed under g.

The first corollary follows from Theorem 3.3 and Corollary 3.4. The second uses Corollary 3.5.

The second corollary gives a method for establishing primitive recursive bounds for computable functions which are defined by means of various combinatorial theorems. To show that a function is bounded by a primitive recursive function, it is sufficient to show that regular initial segments of models of TA are closed under the function. This line of argument was suggested by Paris in [59]: by working in regular initial segments, we have set-theoretic and model-theoretic tools available that are not available in $I\Sigma_1$.

Petri nets were introduced by Petri, and for a full discussion we refer the reader to [67]; vector addition systems were introduced by Karp and Miller [30]. Both Petri nets and vector addition systems are used for modelling problems in parallel processing; for the kinds of problems discussed here, the two concepts are intertranslatable, and we will restrict our discussion to vector addition systems. A vector addition system of dimension k is given by a finite set $V_1, \ldots, V_t$ of vectors in $\underset{\sim}{Z}^k$ and a vector W_0 in $\mathbb{N}^k$. For W, W' in $\mathbb{N}^k$, we write $W \longrightarrow W'$ if $W' = W + V_i$ for some i, and we write $W \leq W'$ if at each coordinate p, $W(p) \leq W'(p)$. A finitely branching tree is associated with the system by the following rules:

(a) W_0 is the root;

(b) if W is a node, the children of W are all W'
     such that

     (i) W $\rightarrow$ W',

     (ii) W $\neq$ W' and for no ancestor W'' of W do
           we have W'' $\leq$ W'.

This finitely branching tree, called the Karp-Miller tree, is
an important tool in the theoretical analysis of vector
addition systems and Petri nets. The key property of the tree
is that it is finite. The proof of this fact proceeds in two
stages. First, by the König Infinity Lemma, if the tree is
infinite, then there must be an infinite path, say $W_0 \rightarrow$
$W_1 \rightarrow W_2 \rightarrow$ ... with the property that $W_i \leq W_j$ implies
j < i. Now the version of the Konig Infinity Lemma invoked
here holds in regular initial segments, since the branching of
the tree is bounded by a primitive recursive function. The
second stage of the argument is to show that an unbounded
sequence W_1, W_2, ... must have i < j such that $W_i \leq W_j$.
Let us look at the argument. Assuming the contrary, for each
pair i < j, there is some coordinate p such that $W_i(p) >$
$W_j(p)$. Now we proceed by induction on the dimension k of
the system. If k = 1, finiteness is immediate since decreasing sequences of non-negative integers are finite. If
k = k'+1, we reduce to dimension k' as follows. Consider
the sequence of first coordinates, $W_1(1)$, $W_2(1)$, $W_3(1)$, ...
and the two cases:

(1) This sequence takes infinitely many values. Then
there is an infinite subsequence such that $W_{i_1}(1) < W_{i_2}(1) <$
... and we can reduce to dimension k'. This pruning argument can be carried out in regular initial segments.

(2) This sequence takes finitely many values. Then there
is an infinite subsequence W_{i_1}, W_{i_2}, ... such that they all
have the same first coordinate; again we reduce to dimension
k'. This is an example of the pigeon-hole principle that can
be used to characterize regular initial segments.

The upshot of this proof of the finiteness of the tree is
that for each dimension k, the function $G_k(\langle V_1, \ldots, V_t, W_0 \rangle)$
which bounds the size of the Karp-Miller tree for the system
V_1, ..., V_t, W_0 is a total recursive function and that
regular initial segments are closed under this function.
Therefore by Corollary 3.9, this function is bounded by a
primitive recursive function. Given the closure properties of
the class of primitive recursive functions, the function G_k
itself is primitive recursive.

We thus have a primitive recursive bound for G_k in each
dimension k. By the work of Mayr and Meyer [51] on the containment problem for finite reachable nets and systems, there
is no primitive recursive bound uniformly in k. In [46], an
analysis is made which is finer than that of the proof we have
just sketched and which yields a bound for G_k in terms of
F_{k+1}; this argument directly exploits the finite Löwenheim-
Skolem intuition.

As a second example, we consider a variant of Ramsey's Theorem. Let $[a,b]$ denote the set of integers a, $a+1$, ..., b. Denote by $[a,b]^n$ the collection of all n-element subsets of $[a,b]$. If P is a map on $[a,b]^n$ which takes k or fewer values, we write $P : [a,b]^n \to k$. In the present context, such a map is called a <u>coloring</u> of $[a,b]^n$ and the function values are called <u>colors</u>. A subset H of $[a,b]$ is called <u>homogeneous</u> for the coloring P of $[a,b]^n$ if P is constant on H^n. For k, m in $\mathbb{N}$, we write $[a,b] \to (*)_k^n$ to mean that for every coloring $P : [a,b]^n \to k$ there is a homogeneous set H satisfying

(i) cardinality of $H \geq n+1$,

(ii) cardinality of $H \geq \min H$,

where $\min H$ denotes the least element of H. To destroy the suspense, for every a, n, k there exists b such that $[a,b] \to (*)_k^n$. For an elegant proof using the König Infinity Lemma and the Infinite Ramsey Theory, <u>cf</u>. [2]. Let us specialize to the case $k = 2$. As the argument that follows will show, the map $R_k(a) =$ the least b such that $[a,b] \to (*)_k^2$ is primitive recursive. The method uses the technology of regular initial segments to replace infinitary arguments as in the previous example. We alert the reader that the sketch of the proof in the next paragraph does suppose a certain familiarity with non-standard arithmetic. The proof is due to Paris [58].

Let M be a non-standard model of TA. What is required is to show that for every regular initial segment $I < M$ and

and every $a < I$ and every $b > I$, we have $M \models [a,b] \rightarrow$ $(*)_k^2$ for each standard k. This will imply that $R_k(a) \leq b$ for all $b > I$ and so $R_k(a) < I$. So let $M \models P : [a,b]^2 \rightarrow k$. Let M' be as in Figure 3 and let c be a new integer interpolated between $I = j(I)$ and $j(M-I)$. Following the Erdös-Rado proof of Ramsey's Theorem (cf. [18]), and working in M', define a sequence x_i as follows: $x_0 = a$; if $i < c-a$ and if $x_0, \ldots, x_i$ is defined, let x_{i+1} be the least $x < c$ such that for all $j \leq i$, $P(x_j, x) = P(x_j, c)$. Let d be the length of this sequence. The claim is that $I < d$, that the sequence is unbounded in I, and that for all $e < I$, the initial subsequence $x_0, \ldots, x_e$ is definable in M and so coded by a Gödel sequence number in M. Admitting the claim, let us see how the proof finishes. The function $P'(x) = P(x,c)$ maps the set $\{x_0, \ldots, x_d\}$ into k classes and k is standard. Therefore, there is a subsequence $y_0, \ldots, y_{d'}$ with $d' > I$ which is unbounded in I and on which P is constant. (Note that I is not necessarily regular in M' and so the hypothesis that k be standard is required here for the piegon-hole argument.) Now set $H = \{y_0, \ldots, y_{y_0}\}$. Since $y_0 < I$ and since $I < d'$, y_{y_0} exists and H is definable in M and so coded as a finite set in M. Thus $M \models [a,b] \rightarrow (*)_k^2$, since H has the required properties and P was arbitrary. So the proof is reduced to the above claim. The claim can be established along the following lines: suppose $x_0, \ldots, x_d$ is bounded in I by $e < I$. Let x_f be the greatest element of the sequence which is less than e. Then $f \leq e$ and the sequence $x_0, \ldots, x_f$ is definable in M. Back in M', the function $Q(x_i) = P(x_i,c)$ maps $\{x_0,\ldots,x_f\}$ to a k-element set; this function is therefore coded as a finite set in M' and in M. Since $M' \models \exists x \forall i \leq f[P(x_i,x) = Q(x_i)]$, this must also hold in M. So let g be the least element in M such that $M \models \forall i \leq f[P(x_i,g) = Q(x_i)]$. But then $g < c$ since M' is an elementary extension of M and g must also be the least element satisfying this property in M'. Thus $g < I$ and $g = x_{f+1}$, contradicting the hypothesis that the sequence was bounded in I.

Thus each function R_k is primitive recursive. On the other hand, as shown in [61] by a direct combinatorial argument, the R_k eventually majorize all the functions F_n. We reach the following conclusion.

<u>Theorem 3.10</u>. The sequence of functions $\{R_k\}$ forms an envelope for $I\Sigma_1$. Thus the statements $\forall x \exists y \, [y = R_k(x)]$ are theorems of $I\Sigma_1$ but the statement $\forall x \exists y \, [y = R_x(x)]$ is not provable in $I\Sigma_1$.

The proof we have just sketched showed that the R_k are primitive recursive functions using models of arithmetic; for a direct combinatorial proof which gives explicit bounds for these functions, we refer the reader to the paper [17] of Erdös and Mills.

We give one further example of an envelope for $I\Sigma_1$. For natural numbers n, k $(n \geq 1, \ k \geq 2)$, define the <u>derivative</u>

164

$(n)_k$ to be the number obtained by writing $(n-1)$ in base k,

$$n - 1 = k^m t_m + k^{m-1} t_{m-1} + \ldots + k^0 t_0,$$

and then replacing k by $k+1$. For $n = 0$, $(n)_k$ is undefined. For natural numbers $n \geq 1$ and $k \geq 2$, we define the modified Goodstein sequence starting at n and at base k by

$$n_1 = (n)_k,$$
$$n_{i+1} = (n_i)_{i+i}.$$

In [23], Goodstein showed that these sequences eventually take the value zero and so are finite in length. (In a moment, we will give explicit bounds on the lengths of these sequences.) Next for $m \geq 1$, define $f_m(s)$ as the length of the modified Goodstein sequence starting at $(s+1)^m$ and at base $(s+1)$.

Note that $(s+1)^m = \underset{m \text{ times}}{(1,0,\ldots,0)}$ in base $(s+1)$ and that the derivative $((s+1)^m)_{s+1} = \underset{m \text{ times}}{(s,s,\ldots,s)}$ in base $(s+2)$. The next lemma will enable us to show that the functions $\{f_m\}$ form an envelope for $I\Sigma_1$ and to exhibit a particularly simple independent statement. The proof of the lemma will be a straightforward computation.

Lemma 3.11. The functions $f_m(s)$ satisfy the recurrence

(1) $f_1(s) = s + 1$,

(2) $f_{m+1}(s) = f_m^{\langle s+1 \rangle}(s) - s$,

where $f_m^{\langle i \rangle} = f_m(s) + s$ and $f_m^{\langle i+1 \rangle}(s) = f_m^{\langle i \rangle}(s) + f_m(f_m^{\langle i \rangle}(s))$.

<u>Proof</u>. The proof is by induction on m. For $m = 1$, the result is immediate. So suppose the theorem holds for f_m, $m \geq 1$; let us compute f_{m+1}. In base $(s+2)$, the number $n_1 = ((s+1)^{m+1})_{s+1}$ is $\underset{m+1 \text{ times}}{(s,\ldots,s)}$. The numbers n_i in the modified Goodstein sequence to be considered will all satisfy $n_i < (s+i+1)^{m+1}$ and so will all be of the form $n_i = (n_{i,0},\ldots,n_{i,m})$ in base $(s+i+1)$. We call a number n_i in this section <u>critical</u> if $n_i = (n_{i,0},0,\ldots,0)$ in base $(s+i+1)$. Suppose n_i is not critical and that $n_i = (n_{i,0},\ldots,n_{i,m})$ in base $(s+i+1)$; let $\bar{n}_i = n_i - n_{i,0} \cdot (s+i+1)^m$. So $\bar{n}_i = (n_{i,1},\ldots,n_{i,m})$ in base $(s+i+1)$. But then we have $n_{i+1} = (n_i)_{s+i+1} = (s+i+1)^m n_{i,0} + (\bar{n}_i)_{s+i+1}$. Thus if $n_{i+1} = (n_{i+1,0},\ldots,n_{i+1,m})$ in base $(s+i+2)$, we have $n_{i+1,0} = n_{i,0}$ and $(n_{i+1,1},\ldots,n_{i+1,m})$ in base $(s+i+2)$ is equal to the derivative $(n_i)_{s+i+1}$. These remarks enable us to apply the induction hypothesis and to deduce that the first critical number in the sequence of the n_i is

$$n_{f_m(s)} = (s,0,\ldots,0) \quad \text{in base} \quad s+1+f_m(s).$$

In other words, the first critical number is

$$n_{f_m^{\langle 1 \rangle}(s)-s} = (s,0,\ldots,0) \quad \text{in base} \quad f_m^{\langle 1 \rangle}(s) + 1.$$

The next number in the sequence is then

166

$$n_{f_m^{\langle 1 \rangle}(s)-s+1} = (s-1, \ f_m^{\langle 1 \rangle}(s), \ \ldots, \ f_m^{\langle 1 \rangle}(s))$$

$$\text{in base} \quad f_m^{\langle 1 \rangle}(s)+2.$$

Continuing to apply the induction hypothesis in this way, we see that the ith critical number is

$$n_{f_m^{\langle i \rangle}(s)-s} = (s - (i-1), 0, \ldots, 0) \quad \text{in base} \quad f_m^{\langle i \rangle}(s)+1$$

and the following number is

$$n_{f_m^{\langle i \rangle}(s)-s+1} = (s-i, \ f_m^{\langle 1 \rangle}(s), \ \ldots, \ f_m^{\langle i \rangle}(s))$$

$$\text{in base} \quad f_m^{\langle i \rangle}(s)+2.$$

The last critical number is the $(s+1)^{st}$ which is thus

$$n_{f_m^{\langle s+1 \rangle}(s)-s} = (0,\ldots,0) \quad \text{in base} \quad f_m^{\langle s+1 \rangle}(s)+1.$$

And so we have $f_{m+1}(s) = f_m^{\langle s+1 \rangle}(s) - s$. $\square$

It is now straightforward to check that $f_{m+2}(x) \geq F_m(x)$. Since the lemma implies that each function f_m is primitive recursive we can conclude that the sequence $\{f_m\}$ forms an envelope for $I\Sigma_1$. In order to give an example of an independence result which is very easy to formulate, we introduce the following function. Let $mg(n)$ be the length of the modified Goodstein sequence staring at n and at base 2. Note that $mg(2^n) = f_n(1)$ but that $mg(2^{n+1}) \geq f_n(2n+1) \geq f_n(n)$ for $n \geq 2$, as is easily verified by induction on n. Putting things together gives the next theorem.

Theorem 3.12

(i) The modified Goodstein function $n \rightarrow mg(n)$ eventually majorizes every primitive recursive function.

(ii) The statement $\forall x \exists y \; [y = mg(x)]$ is not provable in $I\Sigma_1$.

The intuitively surprising fact that the Goodstein sequences are finite in length was proved (in a much stronger version) by Goodstein in [23], who drew attention to the connection between his result and the incompleteness of arithmetic. In [37], Kirby and Paris show, using ordinal arithmetic and the theory of large finite sets of Ketonen and Solovay [31], that Goodstein sequences give examples of independent statement for PA and subsystems of PA. That the modified Goodstein function mg is not primitive recursive can be derived from Theorem 1' of [37]. The direct proof that mg is not primitive recursive by calculating the functions f_m is due to the author and F.S. Beckman. An analogous formulation is due to Cichon [10]. Further work on Goodstein sequences has been done by Abrusci, Girard and van der Wiele [1] in a general proof theoretic framework.

Although we have been emphasizing the role of $I\Sigma_1$ and the primitive recursive functions in this paper, much of the work on envelopes and independence results has been carried out for PA and even stronger theories. As a rather short list of references, we indicate [35,57,61,33,11,20,53,58,13, 30]. To make good on an earlier promise, we state the main result of [61], which gives a characterization of the provably recursive functions of PA.

In the notation of the discussion preceding Theorem 3.10, let $P_n(k)$ = the least b such that $[1,b] \rightarrow (*)_k^n$. The Paris-Harrington result can be stated as follows:

Theorem 3.13

(i) The functions $P_n(x)$ form an envelope for PA; moreover, a recursive function is a provably recursive function of PA if and only if it is primitive recursive in some $P_n(x)$.

(ii) The statement $\forall x \exists y [P_x(x) = y]$ is not provable in PA.

We conclude this section with an application of the machinery we have developed to the question of the possible independence of the P =? NP question. For a related approach in the context of non-standard models of weak systems of arithmetic, we refer the reader to [28] and to [39]. We also refer the reader to [15] and [42].

Let e_1, e_2, ... be a recursive list of the Gödel numbers of all polynomial time bounded deterministic Turing machines.

The assertion P ≠ NP can be formulated as follows:

For every n, there is a propositional formula p̰
such that on input p̰, e_n returns 'satisfiable'
<==> p is not satisfiable.

In this phrasing, P ≠ NP asserts the existence of a recursive function W(n) = p̰ which returns the least witness that
the machine e_n fails as an algorithm for satisfiability.
According to our present lights, W is perhaps a partial
function; to make it total, by convention set W(n) = ∞ if
e_n is in fact an algorithm for satisfiability.

Denote by $\Pi_1(\mathbb{N})$ the set of all Π_1-sentences satisfied
in the standard model $\mathbb{N}$. This set coincides with the set of
all Π_1-sentences in the theory TA. It is not a recursive
set, since the set of Σ_1-sentences of TA is a complete r.e.
set.

Let T be a subtheory of TA and consider the augmented
theory $T + \Pi_1(\mathbb{N})$. The first observation to make is that if
P ≠ NP is independent of $T + \Pi_1(\mathbb{N})$, then P ≠ NP must be
true: for otherwise, for some natural number k we would
have

$$N \models \forall p̰ \text{ [on input } p̰, \ e_k \text{ returns 'satisfiable'} \longleftrightarrow$$
$$p̰ \text{ is satisfiable].}$$

But this formula is (equivalent to) a Π_1-sentence and so
would be a theorem of $T + \Pi_1(\mathbb{N})$. However, assuming P ≠ NP

170

we do have a result on the rate of growth of the witness function W.

Theorem 3.14. Suppose $P \neq NP$ and that $\{f_n\}$ is an envelope for the theory T. Then $P \neq NP$ is independent of $T + \Pi_1(\mathbb{N})$ if and only if the witness function W is not majorized by any function f_n.

Proof. Suppose W is not majorized by an f_n. We show there exists a model of $T + \Pi_1(\mathbb{N})$ in which $P = NP$ holds. Since the witness function is assumed not to be majorized by any f_n, by the Compactness Theorem there is a model M of TA with infinite integer b such that $M \models f_n(b) < W(b)$ for all standard n. By "overspill," for some non-standard a we must have $M \models f_a(b) < W(b)$. By Theorem 3.3, there is an initial segment $I < M$ such that $b < I$ and such that $I \models T$. Moreover, since I is an initial segment of M, I satisfies all Π_1-sentences satisfied in M. Thus I is a model of $\Pi_1(\mathbb{N})$; however

$$I \models \forall \underset{\sim}{p} \text{ (on input } \underset{\sim}{p}, \ e_b \text{ returns 'satisfiable' } \longleftrightarrow$$
$$\underset{\sim}{p} \text{ is satisfiable)}$$

which means that I satisfies $P = NP$.

In the other direction, suppose that W is majorized by some f_k. Then $P \neq NP$ is equivalent in $T + \Pi_1(\mathbb{N})$ to a Π_1-sentence; to check this, let W be bounded by f_k, then

$$\mathbb{N} \models \forall x \forall z \forall u \, [G_{f_k}(x,z,u) \rightarrow \exists y < z \, (y \text{ witnesses that}$$

e_x is not a correct algorithm for 'satisfiability')].

Since $\forall x \forall z \exists u G_{f_k}(x,z,u)$ is a theorem of $T + \Pi_1(\mathbb{N})$, the conclusion follows. $\square$

4. INFINITE INTEGERS AND HIERARCHY PROBLEMS

In this section we shift the emphasis from the global analysis of the structure of models of arithmetic to the analysis of the structure and properties of standard and non-standard integers themselves. From the point of view of Complexity Theory the corresponding shift is from the class of primitive recursive functions and relations to the complexity classes defined by the polynomial time and linear time hierarchies.

In terms of the language of arithmetic, the structure of an integer a in a model M is analyzed by means of the Δ_0-formulas satisfied by a; in other words, by the bounded quantifier formulas $F(x)$ such that $M \models F(a)$. Since the quantification and terms in $F(a)$ involve standard powers a^n, the truth value of $F(a)$ only depends on the structure of M up through some standard power of a. Thus the Δ_0-formulas satisfied by a are determined by the initial segment

$$K_a = \{x : x < a^n, \text{ for some standard } n\}.$$

A suggestive alternative notation for the initial segment K_a is $a^{\mathbb{N}}$. As noted in Section 2, this segment is closed under the addition and multiplication of the model M and so is a

172

structure for the language $\mathbb{L}$.

There are several important "bridging theorems" which connect the study of Δ_0-properties of integers with questions of Complexity Theory. The <u>rudimentary sets</u> were introduced by Smullyan [73] for the study of computability on strings over a finite alphabet. To fix ideas, let S be the alphabet $\{0,1\}$. We recall some definitions. We consider a first-order language with equality, with constant symbols $\underset{\sim}{0}$, $\underset{\sim}{1}$ and $\underset{\sim}{e}$ (for the empty word) and with a binary function symbol $*$ for concatenation. We usually omit $*$ and write xy rather than $x*y$. Thus sample terms are $\underset{\sim\sim}{01}$, $x(yz)$ and $\underset{\sim}{e}x$. We add to this language the "length bounded quantifiers" $\exists |x| \leq |y|$ and $\forall |x| \leq |y|$, which are interpreted as "there exists x of length less than or equal to the length of y such that ..." and "for all x of length less than or equal to that of y ... ." The set of strings S^* together with concatenation and equality provides an interpretation for the language we have just described. A predicate or operation on S^* is said to be <u>rudimentary</u> if its graph is definable by a formula of this language. Smullyan [73] showed that the basic properties and operations of computation on strings are definable in terms of concatenation, equality and length-bounded quantification and thus are rudimentary.

The principal "bridging theorem" between the notions of rudimentary sets of strings and arithmetically definable sets of natural numbers is due to Bennett [7]. A one-one map from S^* to $\mathbb{N}$ is given by the dyadic representation of natural numbers

$$(a_0, \ldots, a_n) \longrightarrow (a_0+1) 2^n + (a_1+1) 2^{n-1} + \ldots + a_n.$$

Bennett's result is that a set of strings is rudimentary if
and only if it is the set of dyadic representations of a Δ_0-
set of natural numbers. A key lemma in Bennett's proof is
that the graph of exponentiation is Δ_0:

<u>Lemma 4.1</u> (Bennett). There is a Δ_0-formula $E(x,y,z)$ such
that, for all natural numbers m, n, k,

$$E(m,n,k) \iff m^n = k.$$

For the proof we refer the reader to [7] or [16]. This
lemma makes it possible to use decoding techniques involving
exponentiation in working with Δ_0-properties; we will see
examples of this below. One corollary easily noted is that
the graph of the logarithm function $y = \log x$, the integer
part of the log of x to the base 2, is also Δ_0.

We will now develop an approach to complexity problems
initiated by Paris and Dimitracopoulos [60] which relates
questions of the linear time and polynomial time hierarchies
to questions on truth definitions for Δ_0-formulas.

The formulas of the language of arithmetic can be coded by
means of natural numbers, associating with each formula F a
Gödel number $\ulcorner F \urcorner$. For our purposes, we shall henceforth
<u>identify</u> formulas with their Gödel numbers. Thus a formula F

174

is a natural number. Technically this will simplify notation.

We will be especially interested in the satisfaction relation

$$\mathbb{N} \models F(n)$$

where $F(x)$ is a Δ_0-formula and n is a natural number. As a subset of $\mathbb{N} \times \mathbb{N}$ this relation is primitive recursive. Thus there is a fixed Δ_0-formula $V(x,y,z)$ such that for all n and for all Δ_0-formulas $F(x)$,

(i) $F(n) \iff \exists y V(n,y,F).$

In (i) we are using the identification of F with its Gödel number.

We address the following question: under what conditions can the unlimited quantifier $\exists y$ be eliminated or even bounded in terms of n and F? The first result we give is a negative one, basically showing that the quantifier $\exists y$ cannot be entirely eliminated.

<u>Theorem 4.2</u> (Weak Tarski Theorem). There <u>cannot</u> exist a Δ_0-formula $V(x,z)$ and functions $F \longrightarrow F^*$, $F \longrightarrow n_F$ such that for all Δ_0-formulas $F(x)$ and all $n \geq n_F$

$$V(n,F^*) \iff F(n).$$

<u>Proof</u>. To reach a contradiction, suppose that the predicate $V(x,z)$ and the above functions exist. Set $S_F = \{m \leq n_F : F(m)\}$. We alter the predicate $V(x,z)$ slightly in order to

175

replace F* by the triple $\langle n_F, S_F, F* \rangle$ by setting

$$V'(x, \langle z_1, z_2, z_3 \rangle) \Longleftrightarrow [(n \leq z_1 \ \& \ n \ \text{is an element of the}$$
$$\text{finite sequence coded by} \ z_2) \lor (n > z_1 \ \& \ V(n, z_3))].$$

Thus, $F(n) \Longleftrightarrow V'(n, \langle n_F, S_F, F \rangle)$ holds for all n. Set $G(x)$
to be $\lnot V'(x,x)$ and n_0 to be $\langle n_G, S_G, G* \rangle$. This gives a
contradiction, namely

$$\lnot V'(n_0, n_0) \Longleftrightarrow G(n_0) \Longleftrightarrow V'(n_0, n_0). \quad \square$$

Following Paris-Dimitracopoulos, we formulate this result
in non-standard terms. The proof is by a compactness argument.

<u>Corollary 4.3</u>. There <u>cannot</u> exist a Δ_0-formula $T(x,z)$ and
function $F \to F*$ which satisfy

$$F(a) \Longleftrightarrow T(a, F*)$$

for all infinite a and all Δ_0-formulas $F(x)$.

Yet another version restates the result in a form which
emphasizes the problem of bounding the quantifier $\exists y$ in the
satisfaction relation. The corollary follows by the simple
remark that $\exists y \leq n^k E(y)$ is equivalent to $\exists y_1 \leq n \ldots$
$\exists y_{k^2} \leq n \ E(y_1 \times \ldots \times y_k + y_{k+1} \times \ldots \times y_{k+k} + \ldots + y_{k^2-k+1} \times \ldots \times y_{k^2})$.

Corollary 4.4. There <u>cannot</u> exist a Δ_0-formula $V(x,y,z)$, a function $F \longrightarrow F^*$ and an integer k which satisfy

$$F(n) \quad \Longleftrightarrow \quad \exists\, y \leq n^k V(n,y,F^*)$$

for all natural numbers n and for all Δ_0-formulas $F(x)$.

In the Weak Tarski Theorem, the role of the parameter n is essential. As will follow from Theorem 4.8 below, there is a recursive (even elementary recursive) map $F \longrightarrow F'$ and a Δ_0-formula $V(x)$ such that the equivalence $F \longleftrightarrow V(F')$ holds for all Δ_0-sentences F. Here and in what follows, we shall use F' to denote the image of a formula F or $F(x)$ under a recursive map.

However, even for sentences there is a version of the Tarski Theorem if we make a sufficient restriction on the map $F \longrightarrow F'$. By a <u>polynomially bounded</u> map we mean a function f such that $f(n) \leq n^k + c$ for some k and c; by a <u>rudimentary</u> map we mean a function whose graph is a Δ_0-relation. If the map $F \longrightarrow F'$ is required to be polynomially bounded and rudimentary, then there <u>cannot</u> exist a Δ_0-formula $T(x)$ which satisfies the equivalence $F \longleftrightarrow T(F')$ for all Δ_0-sentences F. This is proved by a fixed-point argument: for any Δ_0-predicate $T(x)$, with our restrictions on $F \longrightarrow F'$, there is a Δ_0-sentence G such that $G \longleftrightarrow \neg T(G')$; to obtain the fixed-point G one uses the fact that substitution and the other relevant operations on formulas are also rudimentary and polynomially bounded, <u>cf</u>. [73].

Paris-Dimitracopoulos formulate a version of Tarski's
Theorem for non-standard integers, which is not unsimilar to
the version we have just given for Δ_0-sentences.

Theorem 4.5 (Tarski's Theorem for Non-Standard Integers). Let
M be a non-standard model of TA and let a be an infinite
integer in M. Then there cannot exist a recursive function
$F(x) \rightarrow F'$, standard integer k and Δ_0-formula $V(x,y,z)$
which satisfy

$$F(a) \iff \exists y \leq a^k V(a,y,F')$$

for all Δ_0-formulas $F(x)$.

Proof. The initial segment $a^{\mathbb{N}}$ is a structure for $\mathbb{L}$. The
natural numbers $\mathbb{N}$ are an initial segment of $a^{\mathbb{N}}$ and so all
recursive functions are definable in $a^{\mathbb{N}}$, cf [76]. Augment
the language $\mathbb{L}$ with an additional constant $\underset{\sim}{c}$ which we
interpret by a. Assume, in order to reach a contradiction,
that $F \rightarrow F'$, k and $V(x,y,z)$ exist. Note that we then
have a truth definition for Δ_0-sentences of the augmented
language:

$$F(\underset{\sim}{c}) \iff \exists y \leq \underset{\sim}{c}^k V(\underset{\sim}{c},y,F(\underset{\sim}{c})')$$

where $F(\underset{\sim}{c})' = F(x)'$. Recursive functions from $\mathbb{N}$ to $\mathbb{N}$ are
definable in $a^{\mathbb{N}}$ in the augmented language by formulas with
all quantifiers bounded to $\underset{\sim}{c}$. So there is a fixed-point

178

$G(\underset{\sim}{c})$ with quantifiers bounded to $\underset{\sim}{c}$ satisfying

$$G(\underset{\sim}{c}) \iff \neg \exists y \leq \underset{\sim}{c} V(\underset{\sim}{c}, y, G(\underset{\sim}{c})').$$

But then the supposition $G(a) \iff \exists y \leq a^k V(a,y,G(x)')$
fails. □

This last proof is better formulated in terms of a
relational language designed for the structure $\leq a$ of an
integer. Here $\leq a$ denotes $\{b \in M : b \leq a\}$ and the
relational language in question has predicates for the graphs
of successor, addition and multiplication restricted to
integers up to a. We refer the reader to [9] for a more
detailed approach to this topic and to the problem of an
axiomatic treatment of the theory of an integer.

The results we have been discussing are variants of the
classical Tarski Theorem which asserts that there <u>cannot</u>
exist a formula $T(x)$ of $\mathbb{L}$ and an arithmetically definable
function $F \rightarrow F^*$ which satisfy $T(F^*) \longleftrightarrow F$ for all sentences F of $\mathbb{L}$. This is proved by exhibiting a fixed-
point for $\neg T(x)$.

Below we establish some positive results and tie in the
problem of the complexity of the bound on $\exists y$ in (i) with
problems on separation of complexity classes.

For the class of Δ_0-formulas a syntactic hierarchy can be
defined in terms of quantifier alternation:

$U_0 = E_0$ = the class of quantifier-free formulas of $\mathbb{L}$;

E_{n+1} = the class of formulas of the form $\exists x_1 \leq x \ldots$
$\exists x_k \leq xG$ where G is in the class U_n;

U_{n+1} = the class of formulas of the form $\forall x_1 \leq x \ldots$
$\forall x_k \leq xG$ where G is in the class E_n.

Thus a formula in E_k has the form

$$\exists \vec{x}_1 \leq x_1 \forall \vec{x}_2 \leq x_2 \cdots Q\vec{x}_k \leq x_k O(\vec{x}_1,\ldots,\vec{x}_k,x_1,\ldots,x_k,y)$$

where the block $Q\vec{x}_k$ is existential if k is odd and universal if k is even. Clearly, every Δ_0-formula is equivalent to a formula in some class E_k.

It is a long-standing open question whether the sets
defined by the E_k form a true hierarchy [24]. More
precisely, the question is whether for each n there exists
$m > n$ and an E_m-formula $F_m(x)$ satisfying

$$\mathbb{N} \models \exists x(F_m(x) \leftrightarrow\!\!\!/ F(x)), \quad \text{for all} \quad F(x) \quad \text{in} \quad E_n.$$

Naturally this question is related to the problem of the
definability of truth for Δ_0-formulas. The assertion that
the E_n-definable sets form a strict hierarchy is abbreviated
DZH for "delta zero hierarchy."

We now turn to the topic of linear time computation on
Turing machines and a "bridging theorem" due to Wrathall [81]

which connects this model of computation with the Δ_0-sets.

Let L_0 denote the class of languages accepted in deterministic linear time on Turing machines. Following [81], we consider computation relative to oracles with the following convention: oracle queries are written on a special query tape and immediately after a query is made of the oracle the query tape is erased in one unit of time. Proceeding by induction, we let L_{n+1} be the class of languages accepted in linear time by a nondeterministic Turing machine using an oracle from L_n. The sequence of classes

$$L_0 \subseteq L_1 \subseteq L_2 \subseteq \dots \subseteq L_n \subseteq \dots$$

is known as the <u>linear time hierarchy</u>; the assertion that this sequence forms a strict hierarchy, $L_0 \neq L_{n+1}$ for $n = 0, 1, \dots,$ is abbreviated LTH.

The relationship between the linear time hierarchy and the delta zero hierarchy (and therefore between the assertions DZH and LTH) is established by the following theorem of Wrathall [81].

<u>Theorem 4.6.</u> For every n there exist m and k such that

$$L_n \subseteq E_m \subseteq L_k.$$

We refer the reader to [81] for the proof. From this theorem we see that the LTH and DZH questions coincide.

Note that the theorem also shows that the linear time hierarchy is the same as the class of languages accepted in linear time by alternating Turing machines with a fixed finite number of alternations.

The LTH and DZH questions are in turn closely allied to another well known open problem. The _polynomial time hierarchy_ was introduced by Meyer and Stockmeyer [47] in the following terms:

$$\Sigma_0^P = \prod_0^P = \text{the class of languages accepted in polynomial time by deterministic Turing machines;}$$

$$\Sigma_{n+1}^P = \text{the class of languages accepted in polynomial time by nondeterministic Turing machines using oracles from } \Sigma_n^P;$$

$$\prod_{n+1}^P = \text{the class of complements of languages in } \Sigma_{n+1}^P.$$

Clearly, $\Sigma_n^P \subseteq \prod_{n+1}^P$ and $\prod_n^P \subseteq \Sigma_{n+1}^P$. It is an open problem whether the classes Σ_n^P form a strict hierarchy; the assertion that this hierarchy is indeed strict is abbreviated PTH.

By _translating_ Theorem 4.6 _upward_ we can obtain an arithmetic characterization of the sets in the polynomial time hierarchy.

Theorem 4.7. A set of (binary representations of) integers is in the polynomial time hierarchy if and only if the set of integers is definable in $\mathbb{N}$ by formula of the form

$$Q_1 x_1 \leq x^{P_1(\log\ x)} \quad \ldots \quad Q_n x_n \leq x^{P_n(\log\ x)} \quad 0\,(x,x_1,\ldots,x_n),$$

where 0 is a quantifier-free formula and where P_1, ..., P_n
are polynomials.

We shall call the formulas that appear in this theorem the
$\Delta_0(\log)$ formulas, since they are essentially formulas with
quantification bounded by $x^{(\log\ x)^k}$. Again we refer the reader
to [81] for the proof. We remark, however, that this result
can be derived from Theorem 4.6 using "padding" and the fact
that $y = \log x$ is a Δ_0-predicate. As a corollary, note
that the theorem shows that the polynomial time hierarchy
coincides with the family of languages accepted in polynomial
time by alternating Turing machines with a fixed finite number
of alternations. As a further remark we note that this arithmetic characterization of the polynomial time hierarchy does
not require the convention that the query tape be erased after
each oracle call.

The arithmetic characterization of sets in the polynomial
time hierarchy can be finely tuned. For very sharp normal
form results we refer the reader to the paper [27] by Hodgson
and Kent. For an approach which treats the delta zero hierarchy and the polynomial time hierarchy in a uniform way, we
refer the reader to [63].

We now prove some positive results on the complexity of the
satisfaction relation for Δ_0-formulas. To prepare the
groundwork for these results we first describe some

simplifications that enable us to replace an arbitrary E_m-formula $F(x)$ by an equivalent formula that has the form

(ii) $\exists \vec{x}_1 \leq x \ldots Q\vec{x}_m \leq x \exists \vec{x}_{m+1} \leq x$
      $[f(x,\vec{x}_1,\ldots,\vec{x}_{m+1}) = g(x,\vec{x}_1,\ldots,\vec{x}_{m+1})]$,

where g and f are polynomials. To carry out the reduction, starting with a formula $\exists \vec{x}_1 \leq x \ldots Q\vec{x}_m \leq xG(x,x_1,\ldots,x_m)$ with open matrix G, first move all negations in G inside so only atomic subformulas are negated; then eliminate negations, replacing $t_1 \neq t_2$ by $t_1 < t_2 \vee t_2 < t_1$ and $t_1 \not< t_2$ by $t_1 = t_2 \vee t_2 < t_1$. Put the matrix in disjunctive normal form and then eliminate the atomic formulas $t_1 < t_2$ by adding bounded existential quantifiers, for example, by replacing $y < x^3$ with the formula

$$\exists u_1 \leq x \exists u_2 \leq x \exists u_3 \leq x \; (y + x^2 u_1 + x u_2 + u_3 + 1 = x^3).$$

This kind of replacement will work since all variables are bounded $\leq x$ and so all terms can be expressed as polynomials in x. This kind of reduction leads to a formula of the form

$$\exists \vec{x}_1 \leq x \ldots Q\vec{x}_m \leq x \exists \vec{x}_{m+1} \leq x \vee_i (\wedge_j D_{i,j}),$$

where the $D_{i,j}$ are polynomial equations $f_{i,j} = g_{i,j}$. Next we combine the conjunctions $\wedge_j D_{i,j}$ into a single equation by successively pairing $f = g$ & $f' = g'$ into $2\langle f,g \rangle = 2\langle f',g' \rangle$ using Cantor's pairing function $\langle x,y \rangle = (x+y)(x+y+1)/2 + y$ and then by collapsing the disjunction of equations into a

184

single equation by successively transforming $f = g \lor f' = g'$ into $ff' + gg' = gf' + g'f$.

Our first positive result is due to Lessan [40]. It shows, among other things, that the satisfaction relation for Δ_0-formulas is (elementary) recursive. We phrase the result in the form of our question (i) on bounding the quantifier $\exists y$ in terms of n and F.

<u>Theorem 4.8</u>. There is a Δ_0-formula $V(x,y,z)$ and a recursive (in fact, elementary recursive) map $F(x) \rightarrow F'$ such that for all $F(x)$ in Δ_0 and all n in $\mathbb{N}$,

$$F(n) \iff \exists y \leq 2^{(n+2)^{F'}} V(n,y,F').$$

<u>Proof</u>. By our previous reductions, we consider a formula

$$F(n) \iff Qx_1 \leq nQx_2 \leq n \ldots Qx_m \leq n$$
$$[f(x_1,\ldots,x_m,n) = g(x_1,\ldots,x_m,n)].$$

To compute its truth value, we first define a relation R on $(m+1)$-tuples of numbers $\leq n$ by

$$R(k_1,\ldots,k_m,n) \iff f(k_1,\ldots,k_m,n) = g(k_1,\ldots,k_m,n).$$

The values $f(k_1,\ldots,k_m,n)$ and $g(k_1,\ldots,k_m,n)$ are computed recursively according to the way these terms are built up from simpler terms. To capture this recursion in an arithmetic

185

definition, we introduce some notation.

Let $\langle i,j,k \rangle = \langle i, \langle j,k \rangle \rangle$. Then enumerate the polynomials by

$$f_{\langle i,j,0 \rangle} = x_i \qquad\qquad f_{\langle i,j,1 \rangle} = f_i + f_j$$
$$f_{\langle i,j,2 \rangle} = f_i f_j \qquad\qquad f_{\langle i,j,k \rangle} = i \quad \text{for} \quad k \geq 3.$$

With this enumeration, subterms of a term appear before the term itself does. So let $f = f_p$ and $g = f_q$ and $B = \max(p,q)$. Next let A be such that for all $k_1, \ldots, k_m \leq n$ and all $i \leq B$

$$f_i(k_1, \ldots, k_m, n) < (n+2)^A.$$

The computations of the values of $f_p(k_1, \ldots, k_m, n)$ and of $f_q(k_1, \ldots, k_m, n)$ involve values $f_i(k_1, \ldots, k_m, n)$ for $i \leq B$. By the choice of A, for $i \leq B$ we have $f_i(k_1, \ldots, k_m, n) < (n+2)^A$. So the values of $f_p(k_1, \ldots, k_m, n)$ and $f_q(k_1, \ldots, k_m, n)$ are each computed from a sequence of length $< B$ of numbers of size $< (n+2)^A$; such a sequence can be represented by a number in base $(n+2)^A$,

$$S = \sum_{i=0}^{B-1} S_i (n+2)^{Ai}.$$

Note that with this kind of sequence coding, given A, S, $n+2$ and $(n+2)^{AB}$ as parameters, the sequence elements S_i can be

186

decoded in a Δ_0-way using Euclidean division:

$$x = S_i \iff \exists q, q', r, r' < S \; [S = q \cdot (n+2)^{A(i+1)} + r \;\&$$
$$r < (n+2)^{A(i+1)} \;\&\; r = x \cdot (n+2)^i + r' \;\&\; r' < (n+2)^i].$$

This is Δ_0 because all terms appearing on the right-hand side are bounded by $(n+2)^{AB}$; by Bennett's result, the formula $E(x,y,z)$ expressing the relation $x^y = z$ is Δ_0. So $S = q \cdot (n+2)^{A(i+1)} + r$ and the other equations involving exponentiation can be written in a Δ_0-way.

Continuing with the recursive definition of $R(k_1, \ldots, k_m, n)$, we have for all $k_1, \ldots, k_m \leq n$,

$$R(k_1, \ldots, k_m, n) \iff \exists S < (n+2)^{AB} \; [\forall t < B \; (t = \langle i, j, k \rangle$$

$$\rightarrow S_t = \begin{cases} k_i & \text{if } k=0 \quad (k_{m+1}=n) \\ S_i + S_j & \text{if } k=1 \\ S_i S_j & \text{if } k=2 \\ i & \text{if } k=3 \end{cases}$$

$$\&\; S_p = S_q)].$$

The right-hand side of the above equivalence is a Δ_0-formula in the parameters p, q, $\langle k_1, \ldots, k_m \rangle$, A, B and is uniform in F. Call this formula $T(p, q, \langle k_1, \ldots, k_m \rangle, A, B)$. Note that A and B depend recursively on F. To handle the quantifiers we proceed in a similar manner. We define truth-predicates in a recursive way:

$$V_m(k_1, \ldots, k_m, n) \iff R(k_1, \ldots, k_m, n)$$

$$V_{m-1}(k_1, \ldots, k_{m-1}, n) \iff Qx_m \leq nR(k_1, \ldots, k_{m-1}, x_m, n)$$

$$V_{m-2}(k_1, \ldots, k_{m-2}, n) \iff Qx_{m-1} \leq nQx_m \leq nR(k_1, \ldots, k_{m-2}, x_{m-1}, x_m, n)$$

$$\cdot$$
$$\cdot$$
$$\cdot$$

$$V_0(n) \iff F(n).$$

The predicate $V_{m-1}(k_1, \ldots, k_{m-1})$ is a set of sequences of length $m-1$ of numbers bounded by n. Each sequence can be coded by a number bounded by $(n+2)^m$ and the set itself can be coded in binary by a number bounded by $2^{(n+2)^m}$. A fortiori, the other predicates V_i, $i \leq m$, can likewise be coded by numbers bounded by $2^{(n+2)^m}$ and the sequences of length m of these sets can therefore be coded as a number $\leq m2^{(n+2)^m} < 2^{(n+2)^{m'}}$ for suitable m'. The clauses linking the V_i, $i \leq m$, are all expressible by means of bounded quantifier formulas in terms of the parameter $\langle Q_1, \ldots, Q_m \rangle$. This parameter, the quantifier prefix of F, is recursive in F. So we take

$$F' = \langle A, B, m', p, q, \langle Q_1, \ldots, Q_m \rangle \rangle.$$

We can thus obtain a Δ_0-formula $V(x, y, z)$ such that for all $F(x)$ in Δ_0,

$$F(n) \iff \exists y \leq 2^{(n+2)^{F'}} V(n,y,F'),$$

for all n in $\mathbb{N}$. $\square$

The exponential complexity in the bound $\exists y \leq 2^{(n+2)^{F'}}$ is induced by the arbitrary number of quantifier changes from universal to existential that can occur in the quantifier prefix of a formula. If the formulas are restricted to a class E_n, a significant improvement can be made as the next result due to Paris and Dimitracopoulos [60] shows.

Theorem 4.9. Fix m in $\mathbb{N}$. There is a Δ_0-formula $V(x,y,z)$ and a recursive map $F(x) \longrightarrow F'$ such that

$$F(n) \iff \exists y \leq (n+2)^{F'} V(n,y,F')$$

for all n and for all $F(x)$ in E_m.

Proof. First we map $F(x)$ to an equivalent formula of the form (v). This transformation adds an inner block $\exists \vec{x}_{m+1}$ of quantifiers. So we can suppose $F(x)$ is of the form

$$\exists \vec{x}_1 \leq x \ldots Q_m \vec{x}_m \leq x \exists \vec{x}_{m+1} \leq x \; [f_p(x,\vec{x}_1,\ldots,\vec{x}_{m+1}) = f_q(x,\vec{x}_1,\ldots,\vec{x}_{m+1})].$$

As in the proof of Theorem 4.8, we define for $k_1, \ldots, k_{m+1} \leq n$,

189

$$R(k_1, \ldots, k_{m+1}, n) \iff f_p(n, k_1, \ldots, k_{m+1}) =$$
$$f_q(n, k_1, \ldots, k_{m+1}).$$

Exactly as in that proof we determine numbers A, B such that for $k_1, \ldots, k_{m+1} \leq n$ we have

$$R(k_1, \ldots, k_{m+1}, n) \iff$$
$$\exists S < (n+2)^{AB} H(S, n, A, B, \langle k_1, \ldots, k_{m+1} \rangle),$$

where H is Δ_0 and does not depend on F. Since we restrict F(x) to the class E_m, the quantifiers $\exists \vec{x}_1, \ldots, Q_m \vec{x}_m, \exists \vec{x}_{m+1}$ can be handled more easily. The pattern of alternations is fixed by m; only the length of the vectors $\vec{x}_i$ varies. For somplicity's sake we can suppose that all these vectors are of length w, where w depends on F. But, since $k_i \leq n$, this vector can be represented by a sequence of length w of numbers $\leq n$ and thus by a single number $t = \Sigma_{j=0}^{w-1} x_{i,j} (n+1)^{w-1}$. Hence the quantifier block $Q_i \vec{x}_i \leq n$ can be replaced by a single quantifier $Q_i t \leq (n+2)^w$ and the sequence number t is then decodable from the parameters t, n, w in a Δ_0-way. So we have

$$F(n) \iff \exists t_1 \leq (n+1)^W \ldots Q_m t_m \leq (n+1)^W \exists t_{m+1} \leq (n+1)^W$$
$$\exists S \leq (n+2)^{AB} G(t_1, \ldots, t_{m+1}, w, n, A, B, p, q, S).$$

And we can set $F' = \langle A, B, p, q, w \rangle$. $\square$

Putting things together we can obtain a result relating the problem of the complexity of truth definitions for bounded quantifier formulas to the DZH and PTH questions.

Theorem 4.10

(a) DZH fails if and only if there is a map $F(x) \longrightarrow F^*$ and a Δ_0-formula $V(x,y,z)$ such that for all Δ_0-formulas $F(x)$ and for all natural numbers n,

$$F(n) \iff \exists y \leq (n+2)^{F^*} V(n,y,F^*).$$

(b) PTH fails if and only if there is a map $F(x) \longrightarrow F^*$ and a Δ_0-formula $V(x,y,z)$ such that for all Δ_0-formulas $F(x)$ and for all natural numbers n,

$$F(n) \iff \exists y \leq (n+2)^{(\log n+1)^{F^*}} V(n,y,F^*).$$

Proof

(a) $\implies$: If DZH fails, there is a fixed k and a map g that associates with every Δ_0-formula $F(x)$ an equivalent formula $E(x)$ in E_k. So we set $F^* = g(F)'$ where $g(F)'$ is the formula defined by the recursive map of Theorem 4.9.

$\impliedby$: If such a map exists, every Δ_0-set can be defined by a formula of the form

$$\exists y \leq (n+2)^{F^*} V(n,y,F^*).$$

All of these formulas are equivalent to formulas of the same class E_k since the quantifier $\exists y \leq (n+2)^{F*}$ reduces to a homogeneous block $\exists y_1 \leq n \ldots$.

(b) $\Longrightarrow$: By upward translation, satisfaction for formulas in $E_k(\log)$ is expressible in the form

$$E(n) \Longleftrightarrow \exists y \leq (n+2)^{(\log n+1)^{E**}} V(n,y,E**),$$

where $E(x) \to E**$ is recursive. Thus if PTH fails, to every Δ_0-formula F we can associate an $E_k(\log)$-formula $g(F)$ and compose maps taking $F* = g(F)**$.

$\Longleftarrow$: Given a formula of $\Delta_0(\log)$,

$$F(x) \Longleftrightarrow \exists x_1 \leq x^{P_1(\log x)} \ldots Qx_m \leq x^{P_m(\log x)} G(x_1,\ldots,x_m,x),$$

we set

$$H(z_1,\ldots,z_m,x) \Longleftrightarrow \exists x_1 \leq z_1 \ldots Qx_m \leq z_m$$
$$[z_1 = x^{P_1(\log x)} \& \ldots \&$$
$$z_m = x^{P_m(\log x)} \& G(x_1,\ldots,x_m,x)].$$

By Bennett's Lemma the graph of $z = x^{P(\log x)}$ is a Δ_0-predicate. Thus so are $H(z_1,\ldots,z_m,x)$ and the predicate obtained by collapsing the variables into a vector of length $m+1$,

192

$$K(\langle z_1, \ldots, z_m, x \rangle) \iff H(z_1, \ldots, z_m, x).$$

Choosing p sufficiently large, we have

$$F(n) \iff \exists z \le (x+2)^{(\log n+2)^p} \exists z_1 \le z \ldots$$
$$\exists z_m \le z K(\langle z_1, \ldots, z_m, n \rangle).$$

By hypothesis there is a fixed formula $V(x,y,z)$ and a number K^* such that

$$F(n) \iff \exists z \le (n+2)^{(\log n+2)^p} \exists z_1 \le z \ldots$$
$$\exists z_m \le z \exists y \le (\langle z_1, \ldots, z_m, n \rangle + 2)^{K^*} V(\langle z_1, \ldots,$$
$$z_m, n \rangle, K^*).$$

The sets defined by the right-hand side of this equivalence all belong to the same Σ_k^P-class; thus PTH fails. $\square$

In a non-standard setting there is an interesting analogue to this last theorem. The result is due to Paris and Dimitracopoulos [60].

Theorem 4.11. The delta zero hierarchy collapses if and only if there is a Δ_0-formula $V(x,y,z)$ and a recursive map $F(x) \to F'$ such that for all non-standard models M of TA and all infinite $a < M$, we have

$$F(a) \iff a^N \models \exists y V(a, y, F').$$

Proof

==>: Suppose the delta zero hierarchy collapses. If the map $F(x) \to F^*(x)$ which sends every Δ_0-formula to an equivalent formula in some fixed class E_k is itself recursive, then the result follows from Theorem 4.10. If this function cannot be found recursive, the alternative is to use Theorem 4.9 which gives a satisfaction predicate for E_k-formulas along with the fact that the map $F(x) \to F^*(x)$ must be consistent with the clauses of the truth-definitions. In more detail, given $F(x_h)$ of the form $Qx_1 \le x_h \cdots Qx_{h-1} \le x_h$ $[f(x_1,\ldots,x_h) = g(x_1,\ldots,x_h)]$, set

$$F_i(x_1,\ldots,x_h) \iff Qx_i \le x_h \cdots Qx_{h-1} \le x_h$$
$$[f(x_1,\ldots,x_h) = g(x_1,\ldots,x_h)].$$

(The variables x_1, ..., x_{i-1} are exhibited in F_i for uniformity of notation.) To each F_i there corresponds an equivalent E_k-formula $G_i(x_1,\ldots,x_h)$. So by Theorem 4.9, we have, for a_1, ..., $a_h \le a$,

$$F_i(a_1,\ldots,a_h) \iff$$
$$\exists y \le (\langle a_1,\ldots,a_h \rangle + 2)^{G_i} V(y, \langle a_1,\ldots,a_h \rangle, G_i).$$

The set F_1, ..., F_{h-1} is finite but the correspondence $F_i \to G_i$ is not uniquely determined. However, we do have

194

$$F(a) \iff \exists \langle j_i, \ldots, j_{h-1} \rangle \forall i \leq h-1 \forall a_1 \ldots \forall a_h \leq a$$

$$[F_i = \exists x_t \leq x_h F_s \rightarrow$$

$$(\exists y \leq (\langle a_1, \ldots, a_h \rangle + 2)^{j_i} V(\langle a_1, \ldots, a_h \rangle, j_i) \longleftrightarrow$$

$$\exists x_t \leq a_h \exists y \leq (\langle a_1, \ldots, x_t, \ldots, a_h \rangle + 2)^{j_s} V(\langle a_1,$$

$$\ldots, x_t, \ldots, a_h \rangle, y, j_s))$$

$$\& \; F_i = \forall x_t \leq x_h F_s \rightarrow$$

(analogous clause for universal quanitifier)

$$\& \; F_i = (f_p = f_q) \rightarrow$$

$$\exists y \leq (\langle a_1, \ldots, a_h \rangle + 2)^{j_i} V(\langle a_1, \ldots, a_h \rangle, y, j_i) \longleftrightarrow$$

$$T(p, q, \langle a_1, \ldots, a_h \rangle, A, B))].$$

Here $T(p, q, \langle a_1, \ldots, a_h \rangle, A, B)$ is the Δ_0-predicate introduced in the analysis of the satisfaction relation for polynomial equations in the proof of Theorem 4.8; this predicate is "universal" for equations of polynomials. The parameters A, B depend recursively on F. The right-hand side of the above biconditional is thus uniform in the parameters h, $\langle F_1, \ldots, F_h \rangle$, A, B. The recursive map we seek is $F \rightarrow \langle h, \langle F_1, \ldots, F_h \rangle, A, B \rangle$, since the right-hand side of the bi-conditional is satisfied in M if and only if it is satisfied in $a^{\mathbb{N}}$.

$\Longleftarrow$: In this direction we use a compactness argument. We claim that for each Δ_0-formula $F(x)$, there must exist integers $k = k_F$ and $m = m_F$ such that for all $n \geq m_F$

$$F(n) \iff \exists y \leq (n+2)^k V(n, y, F^*).$$

To justify this claim, we argue by contradiction and suppose that it fails. Then there are increasing sequences n_i and k_i of integers such that

$$F(n_i) \centernot\iff \exists y \leq n_i^{k_i} V(n_i, y, F^*).$$

By the Compactness Theorem, there is a non-standard model M of TA with an infinite integer a such that for all standard k,

$$F(a) \centernot\iff \exists y \leq a^k V(a, y, F^*).$$

Hence, $F(a) \centernot\iff a^N \models \exists y V(a, y, F^*)$, which is a contradiction. With the claim established, we can show that all Δ_0-sets are of a bounded complexity: given $F(x)$, $k = k_F$ and $m = m_F$, let $\{s_1, \ldots, s_p\} = \{n < m_F : F(m)\}$. Then

$$F(n) \iff (n = s_1 \vee \ldots \vee n = s_p) \vee (m_F \leq n \ \&$$
$$\exists y \leq n^k V(n, y, F^*).$$

The formula on the right-hand side has the same complexity for all $F(x)$. $\square$

There is a corresponding result for the polynomial time hierarchy.

Theorem 4.12. PTH fails if and only if there is a $\Delta_0(\log)$-formula $W(x,y,z)$ and a recursive map $F(x) \rightarrow F'$ such that for all Δ_0-formulas $F(x)$ and all non-standard a,

$$F(a) \iff a^{(\log\, a)^{\mathbb{N}}} \models \exists y\, W(a,y,z).$$

In Theorems 4.8 and 4.10, the map $F(x) \rightarrow F^*$ is not required to be recursive; however, the definition of satisfaction must hold for all standard n. In the non-standard formulations of Theorems 4.9 and 4.11, the function $F(x) \rightarrow F'$ is required to be recursive but the definition of satisfaction need only be valid for infinite a; put another way, in these theorems the definition of satisfaction is required only to be valid for all standard $n \geq n_F$ where n_F need not depend recursively on $F(x)$.

We now turn to some positive separation results. First we need a definition. Denote by S_k the collection of all Δ_0-formulas of the form

$$Q_1 x_1 \leq x\, \ldots\, Q_k x_k \leq x\, [f(x_1,\ldots,x_k,x) = g(x_1,\ldots,x_k,x)].$$

Thus S_k consists of formulas which contain exactly k quantifiers and whose matrix is a polynomial equation. As we have seen, every Δ_0-formula is equivalent to a formula in some class S_k. The following theorem and its corollary are due to Wilkie [79].

Theorem 4.13. Fix k in $\mathbb{N}$. There is a recursive map $F(x) \rightarrow F'$ and a Δ_0-formula $T(x,z)$ such that for all $F(x)$ in S_k and for all n in $\mathbb{N}$,

$$F(n) \iff T(n,F').$$

The proof of this result uses Nepomnjascii's Theorem ([55]), which shows log-space computable sets to be Δ_0-sets. Wilkie constructs Δ_0-predicates with 33 quantifiers $T^S(F^*,x_1,\ldots,x_s)$ which are universal for open predicates in the sense that

$$0(n_1,\ldots,n_s) \iff T^S(0^*,n_1,\ldots,n_s)$$

holds for open formulas $0(x)$. By placing quantifiers in front of T^{k+s}, similar universal predicates are constructed for all S_k.

Wilkie establishes the following theorem.

Theorem 4.14. The S_n form a strict hierarchy.

Proof. For each n, let $T_n(F^*,x)$ be the universal predicate for S_n-formulas with one free variable. Then $\neg T_n(x,x)$ is a Δ_0-formula which cannot be equivalent to any formula in S_n. $\square$

We remark that in the last proof we do not use the fact that the map $F \rightarrow F^*$ is recursive.

198

Wilkie's Theorem establishes the existence of a strict hierarchy for Δ_0-predicates and thus for the linear time hierarchy. It is a natural question to ask whether there is a direct machine-based or complexity-theoretic counterpart to Wilkie's Theorem for the linear time hierarchy.

Another striking separation theorem for subclasses of the linear time hierarchy has been proved by Paul, Pippenger, Szemeredi and Trotter [66].

Theorem 4.15. The class of those languages accepted in linear time on deterministic Turing machines is properly included in the class of languages accepted in linear time by nondeterministic Turing machines. In other notation, $L_0 \neq L_1$ or $L \neq NL$.

The proof of this theorem of Paul et al. uses a varied collection of techniques from Complexity Theory. Among them is a diagonal argument involving a universal simulator. However, the relation between this result and Wilkie's result has not been analyzed in detail. How the techniques of Paul et al. might apply in the context of the Δ_0-hierarchy has also not been worked out.

Another "bridging theorem" between Complexity Theory and arithmetic is due to Manders and Adelman [48].

Theorem 4.16. The following problem is NP-complete: given natural numbers a, b, c (in binary), do there exist x, y $\leq$ c such that $ax^2 + by = c$?

We refer the reader to [48] for the proof. As a corollary this theorem implies that the class E_1 contains NP-complete sets. For further corollaries and for connections with the Matiyasevich-Davis-Robinson-Putnam Theorem we refer the reader to [79] and [3].

In [81] Wrathall shows that complete sets exist at all levels of the linear time hierarchy. By padding, it follows that for all levels Σ_k^P of the polynomial time hierarchy, there are languages in L_k which are complete in Σ_k^P with respect to polynomial time many-one reductions. Thus, Σ_k^P-complete sets are found in Δ_0, for all k. The following corollary is immediate.

Corollary 4.17. If the delta zero hierarchy is included in Σ_k^P for some k, then the polynomial time hierarchy collapses to Σ_k^P.

We note that this corollary gives an alternative proof of Theorem 4.10(b). Continuing along these lines, the Paris-Wilkie paper [63] cited above contains the following elegant result.

Theorem 4.18. If the delta zero hierarchy and the polynomial time hierarchy coincide, then DZH.

Proof. If DZH fails, then by Theorem 4.10, every Δ_0-set is of the form

$$\exists y \leq (n+2)^{F*} V(n, y, F*).$$

So for each F(x) and all n sufficiently large,

$$F(n) \iff \exists y \le (n+2)^{\log n} V(n,y,F^*).$$

The right-hand side defines sets in Σ_k^P for some fixed k.
By the Weak Tarski Theorem (4.6), this set cannot be in Δ_0.
□

An alternative proof of this last theorem can be given
along rather different lines using Complexity Theory arguments.
We sketch it here to illustrate this convergence of methods.
By Wrathall's work [81], for each k, we have $E_k \subseteq L_{k+m}$,
for some m. Next the strict inclusion $L_{k+m} \subsetneq \Sigma_{k+m}^P$ can be
established as follows: extend Cook's Hierarchy Theorem [14]
to alternating Turing machines with a fixed finite number of
alternations; this can be done by adapting the techniques of
[14], [69] or [83]. Next use the fact that Σ_{k+m}^P is definable in terms of alternating polynomial time machines with
k+m alternations. So we have $E_k \subsetneq \Sigma_{k+m}^P$ and the conclusion
follows.

As we have seen, satisfaction for Δ_0-formulas F(x) can
be uniformly defined using the quantifier $\exists y \le 2^{(n+2)^{F^*}}$;
the PTH and DZH questions have proved equivalent to asking
whether this quantifier can be replaced by
$\exists y \le (n+2)^{(\log n+2)^{F^*}}$ or $\exists y \le (n+2)^{F^*}$, respectively. The
analysis of the gap between exponentiation $2^{(n+2)^{F^*}}$ and
multiplication $(n+2)^{F^*}$ arises here, as elsewhere, as the
central problem of Complexity Theory. In [60], Paris and

201

Dimitracopoulos address the following form of this question: given an infinite integer a in a non-standard model M, does the structure of a determine the structure of 2^a? To make this question more precise, we introduce some terminology.

A map j from $\leq a$ to $\leq b$ is said to preserve the graphs of addition and multiplication if for x, y, z $\leq$ a,

$$x + y = z \iff j(x) + j(y) = j(z),$$
$$x \cdot y = z \iff j(x) \cdot j(y) = j(z).$$

We say that a and b are isomorphic if there is a one-one, onto, order-preserving map from $\leq a$ to $\leq b$ which preserves the graphs of addition and multiplication.

Let us remark that the structure of the initial segment $\leq a$ determines the structure of each power $\leq a^k$, k in $\mathbb{N}$, and so determines the structure $a^{\mathbb{N}}$, which in turn is a structure for the language of arithmetic $\mathbb{L}$. To check this, note that the initial segment $\leq a$ is closed for multiplication of integers $\leq \sqrt{a}$ (where $\sqrt{a}$ is the largest integer whose square is not greater than $\sqrt{a}$) and that $\sqrt{a}$ is definable from a in a Δ_0-way. Furthermore, all integers in $a^{\mathbb{N}}$ can be built up as polynomials in $\sqrt{a}$ with coefficients $< \sqrt{a}$. Thus if a and b are isomorphic, the isomorphism extends to $a^{\mathbb{N}}$ and $b^{\mathbb{N}}$.

So we ask the question whether 2^a and 2^b are necessarily isomorphic if a and b are? Another question is to what extent is the structure of the non-standard integer a (and therefore of $a^{\mathbb{N}}$) determined by the Δ_0-formulas

202

satisfied by a. To simplify the statement of the next result
which addresses the latter question, we introduce some
notation.

For a an integer in a non-standard model M, we set

$$D(a) = \{F(x) : F(x) \text{ is in } \Delta_0 \text{ and } M \models F(x)\}.$$

Theorem 4.19. Let a and b be integers in the model M.
Then a and b are isomorphic if and only if $D(a) = D(b)$.

Proof. From the above remarks, it is clear that if a and b
are isomorphic then $D(a) = D(b)$. For the converse, suppose
that $D(a) = D(b)$. We define a bijection from $\leq a$ onto $\leq b$
by induction. We set $a_1 = a$ and $b_1 = b$. Suppose that
$a_1, \ldots, a_n$ and $b_1, \ldots, b_n$ have been defined and that the
induction hypothesis $D(a_1, \ldots, a_n) = D(b_1, \ldots, b_n)$ is satisfied. Suppose n is odd. Let a_{n+1} be an integer $\leq a$
distinct from $a_1, \ldots, a_n$. Consider the set X of Δ_0-
formulas $\exists x \leq x_1 F(x_1, \ldots, x_n, x)$ such that $M \models$
$F(a_1, \ldots, a_n, a_{n+1})$. For each finite subfamily $\exists x \leq x_1 F_1, \ldots,$
$\exists x \leq x_1 F_s$ of X, we have

$$M \models \exists x \leq a_1 [F_1(a_1, \ldots, a_n, x) \text{ \& } \ldots \text{ \& } F_s(a_1, \ldots, a_n, x)].$$
$$(*)$$

The set X is (identified with) a set of natural numbers;
thus $X \subseteq \mathbb{N} < M$. Since satisfaction for Δ_0-formulas is a
recursive relation, the set X is coded in M; that is,

203

$X = X' \cap \mathbb{N}$ where X' is a definable subset of M. For every finite subset of X, condition (*) is satisfied by $b_1, \ldots, b_n$; so, by overspill, there exists b_{n+1} in M such that for all $\exists x \leq x_1 F$ in X,

$$M \models F(b_1, \ldots, b_n, b_{n+1}).$$

Thus $D(b_1, \ldots, b_{n+1}) = D(a_1, \ldots, a_{n+1})$. Treating integers $\leq b$ at even stages, we can continue <u>back</u> <u>and</u> <u>forth</u> in this way and construct an isomorphism between $\leq a$ and $\leq b$. (Recall that we assume that M is always a countable model.) □

The next result shows that it is possible for non-standard integers a and b to be isomorphic while 2^a and 2^b are not isomorphic. The theorem is due to Paris and Dimitracopoulos [60].

<u>Theorem 4.20</u>. Let M be a non-standard model of TA. Then there exist a and b in M such that a and b are iso-morphic but 2^a and 2^b are not isomorphic.

<u>Proof</u>. Let a be a non-standard integer in M. We first prove that there is b in M such that $D(a) = D(b)$ but $D(2^{2^a}) \neq D(2^{2^b})$. Let c be a new individual constant. Let $D(c)$ denote the set of formulas $F(c)$ where $F(x)$ is in $D(a)$. Consider the theory $PA + D(c) + \Pi_1(\mathbb{N})$, where $\Pi_1(\mathbb{N})$ denotes the set of Π_1-sentences satisfied by $\mathbb{N}$. Call this theory $T(c)$. We claim that for some Δ_0-formula $G(x)$, the

closed formula $G(2^{2^c})$ is independent of $T(c)$. For if not,
for every Δ_0-formula $G(x)$ there would be $F(c)$ in $D(c)$,
A in $\Pi_1(\mathbb{N})$ and P in PA such that either P & $F(c)$
& $A \rightarrow G(2^{2^c})$ or P & $F(c)$ & $A \rightarrow \neg G(2^{2^c})$ would be
provable in the predicate calculus. But this would yield a
definition in M of satisfaction for the formulas $G(2^{2^a})$ as
follows:

$$G(2^{2^a}) \Longleftrightarrow \exists p, P, A(x), F(x) \; [(A, F \text{ in } \Delta_0, P \text{ in } PA) \; \&$$
$$F(a) \quad \& \quad \forall x \leq aA(x) \quad \&$$
$$p \text{ is a proof of } (\forall xA(x) \quad \& \quad F(c) \quad \&$$
$$P \rightarrow G(2^{2^c})) \quad \&$$
$$\text{there is no shorter proof of } (\forall xA(x) \quad \&$$
$$F(c) \quad \& \quad P \rightarrow \neg G(2^{2^c}))].$$

The quantifiers $\exists p, P, A, F$ on the right-hand side can be
bounded by a and, by Theorem 4.8, the clauses $\forall x \leq aA(x)$
and $F(a)$ can be replaced by means of a Δ_0-formula with
quantification bounded by 2^{2^a}. This would yield a single
Δ_0-formula $V(x,y,z)$ such that

$$G(2^{2^a}) \Longleftrightarrow \exists y \leq 2^{2^a} V(2^{2^a},y,G)$$

for all Δ_0-formulas $G(x)$, contradicting the non-standard
version of Tarski's Theorem, Theorem 4.5.

So let $G(x)$ be a Δ_0-formula such that $\neg G(2^{2^{2^a}})$ holds
in M while $G(2^{2^c}) + T(c)$ is consistent. The theory
$G(2^{2^c}) + T(c)$ is a subset of $\mathbb{N}$ which is coded in M. The
collection of subsets of $\mathbb{N}$ which are coded in the model M
forms what is called the <u>Scott set</u> of M or the <u>standard</u>
<u>system</u> of M, denoted in either case by $SS(M)$. In general,
the characteristic properties of Scott sets are closure under
recursive join, "recursive in" and the additional closure
property that every consistent theory in the set has a com-
pletion which is also in the set, <u>cf</u>. [68,40]. Using these
properties and the Henkin method of proof of the Completeness
Theorem, one can construct a model M' of $G(2^{2^c}) + T(c)$
which has the same coded subsets of $\mathbb{N}$ as M; thus $SS(M) =$
$SS(M')$. At this point we need a lemma of Friedman [19].

<u>Lemma</u>. Let M and M' be models of PA which have the same
Scott set and which satisfy the same Π_1-sentences. Then M'
is isomorphic to a proper initial segment of M.

We refer the reader to [19] or [26] for details of the
proof. Basically the proof uses a <u>back-and-forth</u> argument
similar to that in Theorem 4.19 above. The fact that the two
models have the same Scott set is a necessary condition and is
used repeatedly in the proof. Both this lemma and Theorem
4.19 are best understood in the general context of the theory
of recursively saturated models, <u>cf</u>. [40] and [6].

Returning to the proof of the theorem, let j be an
isomorphism for M' onto an initial segment $J < M$. Let b

in M be the image of (the interpretation of) c under this isomormphism; thus $b = j(c)$. Note that 2^{2^c} in M' is sent to 2^{2^b} in M by j; this follows from the fact that j maps M' onto an initial segment of M and thus j preserves Δ_0-predicates. But now in M, $D(a) = D(b)$ since $D(c) = D(a)$ but $D(2^{2^a}) \neq D(2^{2^b})$ since $M \models G(2^{2^b})$ and $M \models \neg G(2^{2^a})$. We finish the proof by remarking that either a and b satisfy the theorem as stated or else 2^a and 2^b do.

We draw a corollary.

<u>Corollary 4.21</u>. Let M be a non-standard model of TA. Then there are integers a, b in M such that $a^{\mathbb{N}}$ and $b^{\mathbb{N}}$ are isomorphic but $(2^{a^{\mathbb{N}}})$ and $(2^{b^{\mathbb{N}}})$ are not isomorphic.

An interesting open problem in this area is whether a isomorphic to b implies $a^{\log a}$ isomorphic to $b^{\log b}$. A positive answer would separate the polynomial time hierarchy and PSPACE, the class of languages recognizable in poly-nomial space, <u>cf</u>. [57].

The above results provide the following picture:

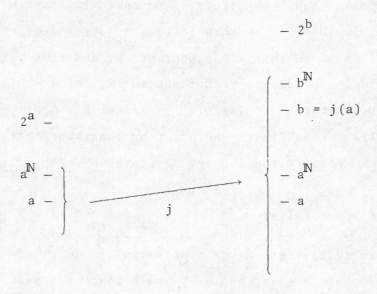

Figure 4

In this picture j is an isomorphism defined up to $a^{\mathbb{N}}$; j is undefined for $x > a^{\mathbb{N}}$; there can be no isomorphism between 2^a and 2^b . However, it might still be possible to have an isomorphism $j : \underline{<}a \rightarrow \underline{<}b$ which extends to an embedding of $\underline{<}2^a$ or of $\underline{<}2^{(a^k)}$ into M. The implications of the existence of embeddings of the latter kind have been studied by Maté in [50].

Let us use the notation $2^{(a^{\mathbb{N}})}$ to denote the initial segment determined by the integers $2^{(a^k)}$ for k in $\mathbb{N}$; that is, $2^{(a^{\mathbb{N}})} = \{x : x < 2^{(a^k)}$ for some standard k$\}$.

Suppose M and M' are non-standard models of TA and that a is a non-standard integer in M. Suppose further

208

that there is a monomorphic embedding $j : \underline{\leq}2^{(a^{\mathbb{N}})} \rightarrow M'$ such that j is an isomorphism on $\leq a$. Thus j maps the initial segment $\leq a$ onto the initial segment $\leq j(a)$. It follows that j maps the initial segment $a^{\mathbb{N}}$ onto the segment $j(a)^{\mathbb{N}}$. For integers c in the interval between $\underline{\leq}a^{\mathbb{N}}$ and $2^{(a^{\mathbb{N}})}$, the map need not send $\leq c$ onto the initial segment $\leq j(c)$ but simply onto a subset of $\leq j(c)$. Under these hypotheses, Maté shows the following fact.

Lemma 4.22

(i) $j(2^a) = 2^{j(a)}$.

(ii) Let T be a (standard) deterministic polynomial time Turing machine; let s be an input string in M for T of length $\underline{\leq}a^k$ where k is standard. Then

$$M \models T \text{ accepts } s \Longleftrightarrow M' \models T \text{ accepts } s.$$

We refer the reader to [50] for the proof of this absoluteness lemma. We do note, however, that since $2^{a^{\mathbb{N}}}$ is not embedded as an initial segment in M', Δ_0-codings cannot be used; Maté uses the Gödel coding which can be expressed in terms of addition, multiplication and existential quantification. The application to be made is seen in the next result.

Theorem 4.23. Suppose M, M', a and j are as above and that for some Δ_0-formula $F(x,y)$ and some $b \leq 2^a$ we have

$$M \models F(2^a, b) \quad \text{and} \quad M' \models \neg F(2^{j(a)}, j(b)).$$

Then NP ≠ co-NP.

Proof. We outline the argument. Toward a contradcition,
suppose NP = co-NP. This hypothesis implies that the polynomial time hierarchy collapses to NP. The binary code for
2^a has length a+1 and the code for b has length $\leq a$.
Denote the code for an integer x by |x|. Since the hier-
archy collapses to NP, there is a polynomial time nondeterministic Turing machine T' such that

$$M \models T' \text{ accepts } \langle |2^a|, |b| \rangle \longleftrightarrow F(2^a, b).$$

Hence in M, T' accepts the string s = $\langle |2^a|, |b| \rangle$. Since
T' is a nondeterministic polynomial time machine, there is a
deterministic polynomial time machine T and a standard
integer k such that for all strings x,

$$T' \text{ accepts } x \iff \exists t, \; |t| \leq |x|^k, \; T \text{ accepts } \langle t, x \rangle.$$

This equivalence is expressible as a sentence of TA. Hence
in M there is a string t of length $\leq |s|^k$ such that T
accepts $\langle t, s \rangle$. By the absoluteness lemma above, in M' it
is also the case that T accepts $\langle t, s \rangle$. So M' $\models$
$F(2^{j(a)}, j(b))$. □

Corollary 4.24. Suppose M, M', a and j are as above and
that D(a) ≠ D(j(a)). Then NP ≠ co-NP, NEXP ≠ co-NEXP, and
so on up through the elementary function hierarchy.

<u>Proof</u>. The hypothesis $D(a) \neq D(j(a))$ implies that for some Δ_0-formula $F(x)$,

$$M \models F(2^a) \quad \text{and} \quad M' \models \neg F(2^a).$$

So the theorem applies and NP is different from co-NP. Now replacing a by $\log a$, which is Δ_0-definable from a, we can reapply the argument of the theorem to $\log a$ and $2^{2^{\log a}} = 2^a$ to obtain NEXP $\neq$ co-NEXP. Iterating this way, one extends the argument to computation classes with time bounds of "stacks of 2's." $\square$

It is not known whether we can "reverse arrows" and show that hypotheses such as NP = co-NP imply that corresponding model-theoretic configurations are necessarily realizable.

It would also be interesting to know if Maté's conditions on the embedding j can be weakened. For example, if we require only that j be defined on $(2^a)^{\mathbb{N}}$ rather than on $2^{(a^{\mathbb{N}})}$, can be conclude that co-NL $\neq$ NL if the truth-value of a Δ_0-formula is changed at 2^a?

Thus far in this paper we have tried to stay clear of the topic of oracle computation. One of the allures of an arithmetic approach is that oracles do not arise naturally. However, oracles are unavoidable--both the polynomial time hierarchy and the linear time hierarchy are defined in terms of oracle computation. Moreover, the characterization of these hierarchies in terms of bounded alternation and Δ_0-predicates shows that the oracle computation is inextricably linked to fundamental questions of Complexity Theory which in themselves do not involve oracles.

In arithmetic, an oracle is simply a set of integers. The language of arithmetic can be augmented by means of a new unary predicate symbol $A(x)$ leading to new atomic formulas $A(t(x))$ where t is a term of the original language of arithmetic $\mathbb{L}$. So if a is an integer and $A \subseteq \mathbb{N}$ is an oracle, the truth value of a bounded quantifier formula $F(A,a)$ depends on a^k and $A \cap \underline{<}a^k$ for some $k = k(F)$. Suffice it to say for now that the Paris-Dimitracopoulos analysis of the complexity of truth-definitions and hierarchy problems can be carried out for oracles--naturally, certain simplifications that we have made do not apply, but no untoward problems arise. The implications of this are not as paradoxical as they might first appear. For example, if A is a PSPACE complete oracle, then $NP^A = P^A$, <u>cf</u>. [5]. Therefore satisfaction for Δ_0^A-formulas must collapse to P^A and thus to $E_n^A(\log)$ for some n. Hence there is a function $F(A,x) \rightarrow F^*$ and a $\Delta_0^A(\log$-predicate $V(x,y,z,A)$ such that for all n,

$$F(A,n) \Longleftrightarrow \exists y \underline{<} (n+2)^{(\log n)^{F^*}} V(n,y,F^*,A).$$

However, by unwrapping the proof that $NP^A = P^A$, one can establish the existence of the map $F(A,x) \rightarrow F^*$ by inspection and one can observe that the map is polynomial time computable in this case.

212

Some very striking work on oracles in a Δ_0-setting has
been done by Ajtai in addressing the parity question: is
there a Δ_0-formula $F(A,x)$ such that

$$F(A \cap \underline{<}n,n) \iff \text{(the cardinality of } A \cap \underline{<}n \text{ is even)}.$$

In [4], Ajtai proves the following theorem.

Theorem 4.25. Let M be a non-standard model of PA^+, an
axiomatizable extension of PA. Let k be a standard integer,
let a be a non-standard integer in M and let R in M
satisfy $M \models R$ is a k-ary relation on $\underline{<}a$. Then there
exists P in M satisfying $M \models P \subseteq \underline{<}a$ & P has even
cardinality and there exist a model M' of PA and a', P'
and R' in M satisfying $M' = P' \subseteq \underline{<}a'$ & R' is a k-ary
relation on $\underline{<}a'$ such that the structures $\langle a,P,R \rangle$ and
$\langle a',P',R' \rangle$ are isomorphic but $M' \models P'$ has odd cardinality.

For the proof, the reader is referred to Ajtai's paper [4].
We draw the corollary concerning the parity question.

Corollary 4.26. There is $\underline{no}$ Δ_0-formula $F(A,x)$ such that
for all $A \subseteq N$ and for all natural numbers n,

$$F(A \cap \underline{<}n,n) \iff A \cap \underline{<}n \text{ has even cardinality}.$$

Proof. Suppose $F(A,x)$ exists. Take M to be a non-
standard model of TA and take PA^+ to be PA plus the
assertion that $F(A,x)$ characterizes even parity for all

finite A. Let a be a non-standard integer of M. Take R to be a relation coding <, plus and times on $\le a$. Then by the theorem there exists $P \subseteq \le a$ in M and a model M' of PA^+ and P', R', a' in M' such that $M' \models F(P',a')$ but $M' \models P' \cap \le a'$ has odd cardinality, which is a contradiction. $\square$

The above application of Ajtai's theorem converges with work of Furst, Saxe and Sipser [21], who have showed that parity cannot be computed by polynomial size circuits of bounded depth.

Ajtai's paper [4] deals more generally with properties of subsets of finite structures that are definable by second-order formulas. We refer the interested reader to [4]. Further applications of these methods to problems close to Complexity Theory have been made by Paris and Wilkie [64,65].

ACKNOWLEDGMENTS
We would like to thank L.A.S. Kirby and Ronald Book for their assistance in preparing this paper. George Wilmers shared with us notes from lectures he gave at the Université Paris VII, which were a valuable help in developing the material in the first half of Section 4.

The research reported here was partially supported by the National Science Foundation under Grants Nos. MCS81-02859 and MCS82-15544.

BIBLIOGRAPHY

[1] Abrusci, V.M., Girard, J.Y., and Van de Wiele, J., Some
    uses of dilators in combinatorial problems, Part I.
    Rapporto Matematico n. 101, Universita di Siena (May 1984).

[2] Aczel, P., Two notes on the Paris independence result.
    Model theory and arithmetic (C. Berline, K. McAloon, and
    J.P. Ressayre, editors), Lecture Notes in Mathematics 890,
    Springer-Verlag (1981), 21-31.

[3] Adelman, L. and Manders, K., Diophantine complexity. Pro-
    ceedings of the 17th IEEE Symposium on the Foundations of
    Computer Science (1976), 81-88.

[4] Ajtai, M., Σ_1^1-formulae on finite structures. Annals of
    Pure and Applied Logic I(1983), 1-48.

[5] Baker, T., Gill, J., and Solovay, R.M., Relativizations of
    the P =? NP question. SIAM Journal on Computing 4(1975),
    161-173.

[6] Barwise, J. and Schlipf, J., An introduction to recursively
    saturated and resplendent models. Journal of Symbolic
    Logic 41(1976), 531-536.

[7] Bennett, J.H., On spectra. Ph.D. dissertation, Princeton
    University (1962).

[8] Cegielski, P., Théorie élémentaire de las multiplication des
    entiers naturels. Model theory and arithmetic (C. Berline,
    K. McAloon, and J.P. Ressayre, editors), Lecture Notes in
    Mathematics 890, Springer-Verlag (1981), 44-89.

[9] Cegielski, P., McAloon, K., and Wilmers, G., Modèles récur-
    sivement saturés de l'addition et de las multiplication des
    entiers naturals. Logic Colloquium '80 (D. van Dalen,
    D. Lascar, and T.J. Smiley, editors), North-Holland (1982),
    57-68.

[10] Cichon, E.A., A short proof of two recently discovered
    independence results using recursion theoretic methods.
    Proceedings of the American Mathematical Society 87(1983),
    704-706.

[11] Clote, P., Weak partition relations, finite games and
    independence results in Peano arithmetic. Model theory of
    algebra and arithmetic (L. Pacholski, J. Wierzejewski, and
    A.J. Wilkie, editors), Lecture Notes in Mathematics 834,
    Springer-Verlag (1980), 92-107.

[12] Clote, P., Anti-basis theorems and their relation to independence results in Peano arithmetic. Model theory and arithmetic (C. Berline, K. McAloon, and J.P. Ressayre, editors), Lecture Notes in Mathematics 890, Springer-Verlag (1981), 134-142.

[13] Clote, P. and McAloon, K., Two further combinatorial theorems equivalent to the 1-consistency of Peano arithmetic. Journal of Symbolic Logic 48(1983), 1090-1104.

[14] Cook, S.A., A hierarchy for non-deterministic time complexity. Journal of Computer and System Sciences 7(1973), 343-353.

[15] DeMillo, R. and Lipton, R., Some connections between computational complexity and mathematical logic. Proceedings of the 11th ACM Symposium on the Theory of Computing (1979), 153-159.

[16] Dimitracopoulos, C., Matijasevich's theorem and fragments of arithmetic. Ph.D. dissertation, University of Manchester (1980).

[17] Erdös, P. and Mills, G., Some bounds for the Ramsey-Paris-Harrington numbers. Journal of Combinatorial Theory, Series A, 30(1981), 53-70.

[18] Erdös, P. and Rado, R., Combinatorial theorems on classifications of subsets of a given set. Proceedings of the London Mathematical Society, Ser. 3, II(1952), 417-439.

[19] Friedman, H., Countable models of set theories. Proceedings of the Cambridge Summer School in Mathematical Logic (A. Mathias, editor), Lecture Notes in Mathematics 337, Springer-Verlag (1973), 113-170.

[20] Friedman, H., McAloon, K., and Simpson, S., A finite combinatorial principle which is equivalent to the 1-consistency of predicative analysis. Logikon Symposon (G. Metiakiades, editor), Amsterdam: North-Holland (1982), 197-230.

[21] Furst, M., Saxe, J.B., and Sipser, M., Parity, circuits, and the polynomial time hierarchy. Mathematical Systems Theory 17(1984), 13-27.

[22] Gödel, K., Uber formal unentscheidbare Sätze der Principia Mathematica und verwandter Systeme, 1. Monatschefte für Mathematik und Physik 38(1931), 173-198. English translation in From Frege to Gödel (J. van Heijenoort, editor), Cambridge: Harvard University Press (1967), 596-616.

[23] Goodstein, R., On the restricted ordinal theorem. Journal of Symbolic Logic 9(1944), 33-41.

[24] Harrow, K., The bounded arithmetic hierarchy. Information and Control 36(1978), 102-117.

[25] Hilbert, D., and Bernays, P., Grundlagen der Mathematik I, II. Springer-Verlag (1934, 1968).

[26] Hirshfeld, J. and Wheeler, W., Forcing, arithmetic and division rings. Lecture Notes in Mathematics 454, Springer-Verlag (1975).

[27] Hodgson, B.R. and Kent, C.F., An arithmetical character-ization of NP. Theoretical Computer Science 21(1982), 255-267.

[28] Joseph, D. and Young, P., Independence results in computer science. Journal of Computer and System Sciences 23(1981), 205-222.

[29] Kanamori, A. and McAloon, K., On Gödel incompleteness and finite combinatorics. Submitted for publication.

[30] Karp, R. and Miller, R., Parallel program schemata. Journal of Computer and System Sciences 3(1969), 147-195.

[31] Ketonen, J. and Solovay, R., Rapidly growing Ramsey func-tions. Annals of Mathematics 113(1981), 267-314.

[32] Kirby, L., Initial segments of models of arithmetic. Ph.D. dissertation, University of Manchester (1977).

[33] Kirby, L., Flipping properties in arithmetic. Journal of Symbolic Logic 47(1982), 416-422.

[34] Kirby, L, McAloon, K., and Murawski, R., Indicators, recur-sive saturation and expandability. Fundamenta Mathematicae CXIV(1981), 127-139.

[35] Kirby, L. and Paris, J., Initial segments of models of Peano's axioms. Set theory and hierarchy theory V (A. Lachlan, M. Srebrny, and A. Zarach, editors), Lecture Notes in Mathematics 619, Springer-Verlag (1976), 211-226.

[36] Kirby, L. and Paris, J., Σ-collection schemas in arithmetic. Logic Colloquium '77 (A. Macintyer, L. Pacholski, and J. Paris, editors), Amsterdam: North-Holland (1978), 199-209.

[37] Kirby, L. and Paris, J., Accessible independence results for Peano arithmetic. Bulletin of the London Mathematical Society 14(1982), 285-293.

[38] Kleene, S.C., Introduction to metamathematics. Princeton: Van Nostrand (1952).

[39] Leivant, D., Unprovability of theorems of complexity theory in weak number theories. Theoretical Computer Science 18 (1982), 259-268.

[40] Lessan, H., Models of arithmetic. Ph.D. dissertation, University of Manchester (1978).

[41] Lewis, H. and Papadimitriou, C., Elements of the theory of computation. Englewood Cliffs, N.J.: Prentice-Hall (1981).

[42] Lipton, R., Model-theoretic aspects of complexity theory. Proceedings of the 19th IEEE Symposium on the Foundations of Computer Science (1978), 176-188.

[43] McAloon, K., Completeness theorems, incompleteness theorems and models of arithmetic. Transactions of the American Mathematical Society 239(1978), 253-277.

[44] McAloon, K., editor, Modèles de l'arithmétique. Astérisque 73, Société Mathématique de France (1980).

[45] McAloon, K., On the complexity of models of arithmetic. Journal of Symbolic Logic 47(1982), 403-415.

[46] McAloon, K., Petri nets and large finite sets. Theoretical Computer Science 32(1984), 173-183.

[47] MacDowell, R. and Specker, E., Modelle der arithmetik. Infinitistic methods (Proceedings of the Symposium on Foundations of Mathematics, Warsaw, 1959), New York: Pergamon (1961), 257-263.

[48] Manders, K. and Adelman, L., NP-complete decision problems for binary quadratics. Journal of Computer and System Sciences 15(1978), 168-184.

[49] Macintyre, A. and Marker, D., Degrees of recursively saturated models. Transactions of the American Mathematical Society 282(1984), 539-553.

[50] Maté, A., Nondeterministic polynomial time computations and nonstandard models of arithmetic. Submitted for publication.

[51] Mayr, E. and Meyer, A., The complexity of the finite containment problem for Petri nets. Journal of the ACM 28 (1981), 561-576.

[52] Mills, G., Models of arithmetic. Ph.D. dissertation, University of California at Berkeley (1977).

[53] Mills, G., A tree analysis of unprovable combinatorial statements. Model theory of algebra and arithmetic (L. Pacholski, J. Wierzejewski, and A. Wilkie, editors), Lecture Notes in Mathematics 834, Springer-Verlag (1980), 248-311.

[54] Mills, G. and Paris, J., Closure properties of countable non-standard integers. Fundamenta Mathematicae CIII(1979), 205-215.

[55] Nepomnjascii, V.A., A rudimentary interpretation of two-tape Turing computations. Kibernetika 6(1970), 29-35. English translation in Cybernetics 8(1972), 43-50.

[56] Parikh, R., Existence and feasibility in arithmetic. Journal of Symbolic Logic 36(1971), 494-508.

[57] Paris, J., Some independence results for Peano arithmetic. Journal of Symbolic Logic 43(1978), 725-731.

[58] Paris, J., A hierarchy of cuts in models of arithmetic. Model theory of algebra and arithmetic (L. Pacholski, J. Wierzejewski, and A. Wilkie, editors), Lecture Notes in Mathematics 834, Springer-Verlag (1980), 312-338.

[59] Paris, J., Some conservation results for fragments of arithmetic. Model theory and arithmetic (C. Berline, K. McAloon, and J.P. Ressayre, editors), Lecture Notes in Mathematics 890, Springer-Verlag (1981), 255-262.

[60] Paris, J. and Dimitracopoulos, C., Truth definitions for Δ_0-formulae. Monograph No. 30, l'Enseignement Mathématique (1982), 319-329.

[61] Paris, J. and Harrington, L., A mathematical incompleteness in Peano arithmetic. Handbook of mathematical logic (J. Barwise, editor), Amsterdam: North-Holland (1977), 1133-1142.

[62] Paris, J. and Wilkie, A., Models of arithmetic and the rudimentary sets. Bulletin de la Société Mathématique de Belgique XXXIII(1981), 157-169.

[63] Paris, J. and Wilkie, A., Δ_0-sets and induction. Open days in model theory and set theory (Proceedings of the 1981 Logic Conference, Poland) (W. Guzicki, W. Marek, A. Relc, and C. Rauszer, editors) (1981), 237-248.

[64] Paris, J. and Wilkie, A., Counting problems in bounded arithmetic. Submitted for publication.

[65] Paris, J. and Wilkie, A., Δ_0-approximations to the counting functional. Submitted for publication.

[66] Paul, W., Pippenger, N., Szemeredi, E., and Trotter, W., On determinism versus non-determinism and related problems. Proceedings of the 24th IEEE Symposium on the Foundations of Computer Science (1983), 429-438.

[67] Peterson, J., Petri net theory and the modeling of systems. Englewood Cliffs, N.J.: Prentice-Hall (1980).

[68] Scott, D., Algebras of sets binumerable in complete extensions of arithmetic. Proceedings of Symposia in Pure Mathematics 5, American Mathematical Society (1962), 117-122.

[69] Seiferas, J., Fischer, M., and Meyer, A., Separating non-deterministic time complexity classes. Journal of the ACM 25(1978), 146-167.

[70] Shepherdson, J.C., A non-standard model for a free variable fragment of number theory. Bulletin de l'Académie Polonaise des Sciences 12(1964), 79-86.

[71] Skolem, Th., Peano's axioms and models of arithmetic. Mathematical interpretation of formal systems (L.E.J. Brouwer, E.W. Beth, and A. Heyting, editors), Amsterdam: North-Holland (1955), 1-14.

[72] Skolem, Th., Begrüdung der elementaren Arithmetik durch die rekurriende Denkweise ohne anwendung scheinbarer Veränderlichen mit unendlichem Ausdehnungsbereich. Videnskapselskapets skrifter, I, Matematisk-naturvidenskabelig klasse, No. 6. English translation in From Frege to Gödel (J. van Heijenoort, editor), Cambridge: Harvard University Press (1967), 302-333.

[73] Smullyan, R., Theory of formal systems. Annals of Mathematics Studies 47, Princeton: Princeton University Press (1961).

[74] Stockmeyer, L., The polynomial time hierarchy. Theoretical Computer Science 3(1977), 1-22.

[75] Tarski, A., Der Wahrheitsbegriff in der formalisierten Sprachen. Studia Philosophica 1(1936), 261-405.

[76] Tarski, A., Mostowski, A., and Robinson, R., Undecidable theories. Amsterdam: North-Holland (1953).

[77] Tennenbaum, S., Non-archimedean models for arithmetic. Notices of the American Mathematical Society 6(1959), 207.

[78] Wilkie, A., Some results and problems on weak systems of arithmetic. Logic Colloquium '77 (A. Macintyre, L. Pacholski, and J. Paris, editors), Amsterdam: North-Holland (1978), 285-296.

[79] Wilkie, A., Applications of complexity theory to Δ_0-definability problems in arithmetic. Model theory of algebra and arithmetic (L. Pacholski, J. Wierzejewski, and A. Wilkie, editors), Lecture Notes in Mathematics 834, Springer-Verlag (1980), 363-369.

[80] Wilmers, G., Bounded existential induction. Submitted for publication.

[81] Wrathall, C., Rudimentary predicates and the linear time hierarchy. SIAM Journal on Computing 7(1978), 194-209.

[82] Woods, A., Some problems in logic and number theory and their connections. Ph.D. dissertation, University of Manchester (1981).

[83] Zak, S., A Turing machine time hierarchy. Theoretical Computer Science 26(1983), 327-333.

Kenneth McAloon
Department of Computer and Information Science
Brooklyn College
City University of New York
Brooklyn, New York 11210, U.S.A.

Index

A

almost everywhere, 18
almost polynomial time algorithms, 82
approximate algorithms, 82
approximation-modulus pair, 15
arithmetic relation, 122
arithmetically definable, 122, 123
arithmetization, 128

B

Bennett's Theorem, 173
binary convergence, 6
binary expansion representation, 7

C

Cauchy sequence representation, 6
census function, 71
closed term, 121
coloring, 162
complete sets, 71
complexity of numerical operations, 20
complexity of real functions, 3
computable numerical functional, 23
computable operator, 24
computable real function, 10, 11
computable real number, 5
computational complexity of real functions, 10
computational complexity of real numbers, 4
conjunctive self-reducibility, 85
counting Turing machine, 32
critical number, 166

D

delta-zero hierarchy, 180
dense sets, 71
derivative $(n)_k$, 164, 165
derivatives, 34
disjunctive self-reducibility, 84
distribution independent, 19

224